BUSINESS
AND
SOCIETY IN
CHANGE

DANIEL P. MOYNIHAN
HANS J. MORGENTHAU
IRVING KRISTOL
DANIEL BELL
ELI GINZBERG
W. WALTER MENNINGER
PETER F. DRUCKER
HENRY L. DIAMOND
CARL E. BAGGE
RONALD ABLER
ROBERT JASTROW

BUSINESS
AND
SOCIETY IN
CHANGE

American Telephone and Telegraph Company

International Standard Book Number: 0-88439-002-2

Library of Congress Catalog card number: 75-869

Printed in U.S.A.

CONTENTS
❧

FOREWORD by PAUL M. LUND

INTRODUCTION by IRVING KRISTOL

THE SOCIAL RESPONSIBILITY OF BUSINESS
DANIEL P. MOYNIHAN, 7

POWER SHIFTS IN AMERICAN DEMOCRACY
HANS J. MORGENTHAU, 27

AMERICANS AND THEIR CITIES
IRVING KRISTOL, 45

CHANGING INFLUENCES IN AMERICAN LIFE
DANIEL BELL, 65

NEW PATTERNS IN THE LABOR FORCE
ELI GINZBERG, *85*

THE MEANING OF MORALE:
A Peace Corps Model
W. WALTER MENNINGER, *97*

PRODUCTIVITY AND
THE KNOWLEDGE WORKER
PETER F. DRUCKER, *111*

THE ENERGY-ENVIRONMENT INTERFACE
HENRY L. DIAMOND, *129*

THE CHANGING REGULATORY SCENE
CARL E. BAGGE, *143*

SETTLEMENT GEOGRAPHY AND
TELECOMMUNICATIONS:
The Next Twenty Years
RONALD ABLER, *155*

THE COMING OF THE GOLDEN AGE:
The Impact of Science on Human Affairs
ROBERT JASTROW, *181*

INDEX *195*

FOREWORD

T HIS book is a collection of some of the talks given to managers in the Supplemental Training Program at AT&T from
1971 until early 1974. The program invited speakers to
share their ideas with AT&T managers in order to help us develop
a better understanding of forces outside the telephone company
that affect it.

The speakers do not reflect the opinions of AT&T, and as a group
they often disagree. They were chosen for their competence in
fields outside the telephone industry and not because they agree
with one another or with Bell System management. What the
speakers offer are some informed and lively views of our contemporary problems and the forces reshaping society.

It is our hope that readers of this volume will find the ideas
and the analysis by these leading thinkers as interesting as our
employees did. We also hope that you, the reader, will see the
presentations as a worthwhile effort to increase common understanding of basic socioeconomic trends among businessmen, educators, and the reading public.

PAUL M. LUND
Vice President
American Telephone and Telegraph Company

BUSINESS
AND
SOCIETY IN
CHANGE

INTRODUCTION

I N marital quarrels one of the major sources of difficulty is that each partner thinks he or she understands the other very well, and is irritated that the other does not also make the effort to understand. What is usually the case, of course, is that neither partner really understands the other at all, and understands himself only partially, and the mutual recriminations are like battleships that pass in the night, firing blindly and indiscriminately into the darkness.

Something of the sort appears to be operating today in the relations between the private and the public sectors of American democracy. Specifically, in the relations between business and government, and most particularly in the relations between the large corporation on the one hand and its academic and political critics on the other. These two components of American life are married to each other, really cannot get along without one another, yet so often end up in an adversary relationship. And this is not an instance—as in the relationship between government and the media, or in the judicial process generally—where it is possible to claim that an adversary relationship is normal and desirable. No one makes such a claim; instead, each of the parties to this quarrel insists that it is entirely the other's fault. As is most often the case in such situations, both sides cannot be right—but both can assuredly be wrong.

Two facts lie at the heart of this controversy. The first is that the large corporation exists, is clearly indispensable to the economic and social well-being of the American people, and is not going to vanish at the wave of anyone's wand. (Even when a large corporation is nationalized, it remains a large corporation in all its crucial aspects—except that it will probably be less efficient.) Second, the genesis of the large corporation is one of those historical events that has never been adequately confronted by political and social theory, and the place of the corporation in American democracy has therefore never been clearly defined. This latter point both needs and merits some explanation.

The social-political-economic system which we call liberal-democratic capitalism was firmly established in this country even before the American Revolution, and its legitimacy has never been seriously questioned. One of its sovereign assumptions was the belief that economic growth and prosperity—and the social stability it engendered—would best be accomplished if the citizen's economic activities suffered as little interference as possible from government. The exact degree of interference that was permissible was always a matter of some dispute. Government never subscribed to the doctrines of laissez faire and "free enterprise" in their most extreme forms. Nevertheless, Americans have generally felt that the burden of proof was upon government if it wished to interfere with the workings of the free market.

All this was part of the profound American belief in the value of individualism and the importance of personal liberty. But note: It was the individual farmer and businessman whose rights were recognized and respected. With the rather abrupt advent of the large corporation in the period 1880–1900, the picture became confusing. No one quite knew how this novel institution—unanticipated by both the Founding Fathers and Adam Smith—fitted into the ideological preconceptions of American democratic capitalism.

The business leaders who were at the head of these new large corporate enterprises cheerfully asserted that nothing fundamental had changed. Business was still business, the marketplace still the marketplace, the large corporation was nothing but the entrepreneur writ large, and "free enterprise" was alive and well, even though in a modernized version. This claim was never really accepted by the public, and is not accepted today—though many corporate executives still believe it and say it. The large corporation is seen as so powerful, so permanent, so consequential an institution, that the claim to entrepreneurial status has never been quite credible. Americans are probably no more antibusiness or anti-free-enterprise today than they have ever been. This is revealed by public opinion polls, which show that the American people have a consistently high regard for *small* business. Their problem is that they do not know where to "place" the large corporation within the business spectrum. Their inclination is to regard it as a species of "private government," and to direct toward it the hostility that Americans have always felt for government that is not sufficiently responsive to the popular will.

When they were first confronted with the large corporation, the nation's political and intellectual leaders were generally confused, suspicious, or downright hostile. With only a few exceptions they have remained so. In part this was because they perceived it as an institution which competed in size, complexity, and influence with the institutions of popular government itself. But too, it was because the idea of the large corporation was not present in their traditional vision of the ideal American republic. And so their instinct has always been to try to abolish it; and if this was not possible, to circumscribe and delimit its activities; and if this was not possible—well then, to harass it in an arbitrary and persistent way. Essentially the hope was that the large corporation would go (or could be made to go) away.

But the large corporation could not go away if it wanted to. It came into existence for good and necessary reasons, those having to do not only with the efficiencies of scale that an urbanized and technologically innovative society demanded, but with the relative stability of employment and economic operations that such a society demanded. Any serious effort to break up the large corporations would have huge economic costs that the average citizen, in his capacity as consumer, would find intolerable. It would also have huge social costs that the average citizen, in his capacity as employee, would be unwilling to pay. Think of the so-called "fringe benefits," such as pensions, medical insurance, profit-sharing plans, which could not exist without the large corporation. Imagine how the trade unions would react to any suggestion that employees forgo them, as employees frequently do in small businesses.

So it is no exaggeration to say that for the past seventy-five years, the dialogue between the corporation and the American polity has largely been what the French call a *dialogue des sourds*—a dialogue of the deaf. Corporate leaders have kept insisting that their institution is perfectly congruent with American traditional ideals of a good society, and critics of the corporation have kept insisting that it is utterly incompatible with those ideals. But the plain fact is that it was simply never envisaged by the traditional ideals. It emerged naturally, it is here to stay, and it requires of us a creative adaptability in both theory and practice which we have not yet seriously attempted.

This is not to say that no one has given serious thought to the question of the corporation's responsibility to society and society's responsibility to the corporation. There have been some objective attempts at answers, but fewer than we need. The dominant tone has remained querulous and polemical. Recently, however, there have been indications that the issue may at last receive the thoughtful and sustained consideration it merits. This collection of informal talks by scholars to corporate employees, sponsored by a major corporation, is one such sign. The talks deal essentially with the question of the relation between the private and public sectors of our democracy—and *this,* rather than "the corporation *versus* government" or "the corporation *versus* the people," is the real issue we must explore. Americans today are citizens of both sectors; basically we accept our dual citizenship and have no desire to opt for one against the other. What do remain to be clarified are the proper boundaries of these sectors and the conditions of their coexistence. Though clarification is long overdue, it is hard to believe—impossible to believe—that it is beyond our powers to achieve.

Irving Kristol

THE SOCIAL
RESPONSIBILITY
OF BUSINESS

DANIEL P. MOYNIHAN

Daniel P. Moynihan, who became U.S. ambassador to India in 1973, resigned in 1975 to resume teaching at Harvard University, where he is professor of government. His government experience includes service as secretary to the governor of New York State (1955–1958), assistant secretary of labor in Washington (1963–1965), urban affairs assistant to the President and a member of the cabinet (1969–1970), and consultant to the President (1971–1973). Moynihan went to public and parochial schools in New York City and took his degrees at Tufts University and the Fletcher School of International Law and Diplomacy.

W HAT is the role of our corporations in the political, social, and economic life of the nation? Americans tend to ask this question approximately every twenty years. There was the period of reappraisal that preceded the Sherman Antitrust Act of 1890, the period of Wilson's first administration, when the Federal Trade Commission was created, and the Roosevelt era, with the SEC and similar forms of regulation. Then it was thirty years—possibly too long—before the subject appeared again in the late 1960s. But I think there's a difference this time around, and that's what I want to talk about.

The general perspective which I am going to offer you is a vista of the decline of authority in late capitalism. By late capitalism I mean the period a century or so after the onset of intensive industrialization, when really large accumulations of economic power and resources became lodged in stable corporate institutions.

Not that new corporations don't come into existence. They do, regularly. Not that some of them don't become large. Some do. But all in all, the situation is fairly stable. We haven't had any new automobile companies now for about forty years. We've got three and a half, and that's about what we're going to have. We've got one telephone company and a few little ones around. We've got three or four big chemical producers and two sugar makers.

I'm not describing monopoly conditions; I'm just saying that these situations are stable. Business churns, corporations start up all the time, there's lots of enterprise in our society. On the other hand, the dominance of a certain number of large banks, large companies, and so on, is the state of a mature or late capitalism. These corporations are now in their second and third generation of leadership.

By the term *authority* I simply mean people's sense of the legitimacy, the appropriateness of certain arrangements for running things. It is a hard idea to get across. When I begin talking to my students about authority and authority relations, right away they don't like it. They associate the word authority with "authoritarian"

—with institutions which make people do what they don't want to do, or ought not to do. But that is not my meaning.

I'm saying that there are roughly two kinds of relationships within a society: power relationships, which are coercive, and authority relationships, which are essentially voluntary. In authority relationships people do things because they sense the appropriateness of doing them. They take direction, they follow leads, because they wish to. In a manner of speaking, the difference between authority relationships and power relationships is the difference between a traffic light and a policeman standing at the intersection. Whereas the policeman regulates traffic by the implicit threat of his club, the light does the same job simply because people agree to stop on the red and go on the green.

A VOTE OF NO CONFIDENCE

One of the most dramatic inventions of our time, and I suppose the largest single achievement of social scientists, is the public opinion poll. It may not strike you as being all that much, but it's the biggest thing we've done and we're very proud of it. Polling has been going on for about thirty-five years now. Although we can't say what people thought of the world in 1870, we know quite a bit about what they were thinking in 1945.

One of the trends that emerges with great clarity in the polls of the past decade is a sharp and steady decline in confidence in our major social institutions. Harris surveys that were begun in 1966 show a downward trend among members of the public who were asked what confidence they had in the people running various institutions. The decline occurred regardless of factors like social class, geographic location, race, or sex. Different groups may have had different reasons for their increasing coolness toward the establishment, but the result has been a general frost.

You won't be startled to hear that one of the largest slumps in confidence was in the military. In 1966, 62 percent of the people who were polled had faith in military leaders. In 1974 the figure was 33 percent, a drop of 29 points. After all, we kind of lost a war—a war that I don't think the military wanted to fight, but they wind up getting the blame. I guess it's fair, since they'd have taken the credit if they had won.

As for other institutions, organized religion dropped from 41 percent down to 32. At the bottom I was surprised to see organized labor: it sank from 22 to 18. The others at the bottom of the list in 1974—both also at 18 percent—were Congress and law firms, which perhaps is understandable.

The institution which the American people rank at the top of the list has shaken my own confidence in them. I had always believed in their general ability to judge performance, but the institution that they continue to respect is the medical profession. Their opinion of it has declined from 72 to 50 percent confidence, but that puts doctors way ahead of anyone else. Perhaps you can explain it.

The decline in confidence in our major companies has been steepest of all: from 55 percent in 1966 to 21 percent in 1974. That's a drop of 34 points among the general population, and the erosion of confidence is sharpest in young people. Very young people appear to have no faith at all in business. And the things they say that business has done worst are precisely the things that business has been doing pretty well in the last ten years. There is a nonrational quality to their disapproval; it does not reflect effort or performance.

What's really behind this loss of confidence? The usual, and often the sensible, approach in such cases is to try and find explanations in the immediate environment, but I don't think it helps a lot here. For instance, in the 1960s we looked for explanations of student unrest in circumstances like the war in Vietnam. Unquestionably the war was one of the proximate causes; yet the fact that the same unrest occurred in France, Japan, and other countries that were fighting no wars suggests the existence of some underlying commonality.

ORDEAL BY RATIONALISM

I believe that the basic connection among these phenomena can be found in Joseph Schumpeter's analysis of capitalist decline, which he set forth in the late 1930s and published in 1942 in his book *Capitalism, Socialism, and Democracy.* Schumpeter was an Austrian, a minister of finance in Austria after World War I, a great economist, perhaps an even greater sociologist. In his commentary on the Marxian view of capitalism, he wrote both to praise Marx and to bury him. Schumpeter said that Marx taught us to see the world in an important new way, but that he was all wrong about capitalism and how it would develop. Capitalism is not going to lead to increasing misery for the masses, to wars for colonial exploitation and foreign markets.

Yet although Marx's version of the evolution of capitalism is nonsense, Schumpeter said, Marx was right when he predicted that capitalism will eventually do itself in. Then Schumpeter stated what he called his paradoxical conclusion: that capitalism will be destroyed by its success. We don't quite know why he arrived at this conclusion, except that it's basically a psychological explanation of behavior.

According to Schumpeter, the great style of capitalism is rationality. The rationalist mode successfully delegitimated—stripped of authority (he doesn't use that term, but I believe he would agree to it)—all the preceding institutions of society: feudalism, organized religion, the monarchy, the guilds. In attacking the monarchy, for example, the rationalist's basic approach would be: "Who appointed you king? How did you get to be king?" The king's answer would be: "God made me king." But the rationalist would bore in: "Who's God? Where is he? Show him to me; I can't see him. Do you have any evidence? Do you have a contract with God?" And pretty soon the fellow didn't really feel he was king any more. And neither did anybody else.

Rationalism brought us into the familiar eighteenth- and nineteenth-century world where bourgeois institutions, as Schumpeter would call them, were dominant. But, he said—and this is the key point—the nonrational aspects of society do not end when rationalism triumphs. Nonrational impulses exist in all of us, though under capitalism they assume a rationalist garb. In the name of rationalism we then begin to attack and delegitimate our institutions.

We say: "Who made the Bell Telephone Company a monopoly? Who gave them that right? Why?" Then we go on to: "Why should there be corporations in the first place?" Once these questions are asked, there are no satisfactory answers—particularly if the impulse to ask them arises not from an inquiring spirit but from the desire to destroy. I believe that Schumpeter regarded this desire as an impulse which is let loose when people abandon a traditionalist society.

Schumpeter declared that capitalism stands its trial before judges who have the sentence of death in their pockets. The only concession that a successful defense can achieve is a change in the indictment. In his opinion, you're not going to get out of that court alive!

Schumpeter even named the group who will be the key agents in the process of destruction. He said that it is the intellectual class who will attack and demolish capitalism. According to Schumpeter, the unique capacity and quality of capitalism will be to finance this class—and the angrier the intellectuals become, the more power they will be given to become even angrier. Schumpeter thought of the intellectual class as being composed of journalists, even though he taught at Harvard for many years. As a Central European economist-statesman, he was used to a tradition of journalist-intellectuals.

THE NORMATIVE STYLE

It seems to me that intellectuals do have an approach that is fundamentally different from most people's—certainly from the operating businessman's. What the intellectual is mostly concerned with are values. He is not interested in market values, in the sense that value resides in what everybody wants. His province is values as the end result of a form of analysis which leads to some judgment about what's good and what's bad. And the intellectual proceeds on the principle that social institutions should reflect values.

The characteristic institution of the intellectual—say, the church or the university—is fundamentally different in its management, organization, and purposes from the characteristic market institution—the corporation. Amitai Etzioni of Columbia University has made a distinction between two basic organizational forms. One he calls utilitarian, the other normative. The great style of the American business corporation is utilitarian. In a corporate structure, people's purposes are clearly defined and their aggression is freely expressed. As an employee you know what you want: You want to go up in the organization, you want to make more money, and you want the organization to make money, which it does by meeting market needs. People don't have to be devious, because they can say exactly what they want—they want the corporation to make money so they can make money. Period.

But in a normative institution everything must be done through indirection, because its members can't express personal aggression and personal ambition. Aggression does not diminish in normative organizations; it just takes different forms. At the Congress of Vienna, Metternich was awakened in the middle of the night to be told that the Russian ambassador had just dropped dead. He rubbed his eyes and said, "Now, what can have been his motive?" That's the kind of reasoning you learn at faculty meetings, not board meetings.

The basic distinction between a utilitarian and a normative institution is that the utilitarian body is primarily concerned with giving people what they want, the normative with giving them what they need. H. L. Mencken said, "Nobody ever went broke underestimating the taste of the American people." In effect the business corporation says: "We produce what people want; they'll pay for it; that's the point." The normative institution says: "Our job is to raise people's taste, to improve their culture, to do for them what they need done, whether they know it or not."

So the normative institution tells people: "I'll explain what's good for you; then you'll do it. If you obey, you will be happy; if you don't, I will . . ." Normative societies can be very unpleasant places to live.

As capitalism succeeds, as people in general get to be pretty well off, more and more of them evolve life-styles that are basically normative. Young people who follow the standard ivy league style today are extremely careful about expressing individual ambition or any sort of personal aggression. They are alert to sense what the group thinks, and their speech has a nonverbal quality: "Well, you know, like, you know, man." How extraordinarily different from Dick Stover in his day! He was out to get the contract, get the job, make the dollar—even though he might leave it to Yale later. This profound transformation from utilitarian to normative standards is a familiar one in history. Upper classes always tend to behave in the current ivy league style.

So the success of capitalism is doing what Schumpeter predicted: it is increasingly diminishing the capitalist's function in the system. You've got Bell Telephone, and it works, sort of—or it used to work. The organizational energy that went into creating the telephone company isn't so important any more, because it's much easier to keep a system going than to start it up. So we've got a telephone system; what can go wrong? But since we've got it, who needs it? Though we'd miss it very much if we didn't have it, plenty of people don't know that.

The problem, I believe, is that a time arrives when a society is at a critical balance in development. A new class is coming along with new demands—in our case, demands for normative behavior by institutions. The demands are in conflict with the previous dominant institutions—in our case, the utilitarian business corporation. Then the new class reaches critical proportions, critical mass, and things begin to happen.

This pattern is visible in all sorts of areas—in local party politics, for example. I was raised in the Democratic party in New York City, when the party members had very little of what you would call social vision. They were concerned with looking after people in the short run, and the problems they worked on had plain utilitarian solutions. People wanted jobs, or they wanted to get out of jail, or they wanted to avoid being put in jail, or they wanted safe streets or sidewalk inspectors.

This utilitarian Tammany approach was assaulted as fundamentally immoral by the reform Democrats, a group of fundamentally upper-class people in the city. Because I lived a little bit in both worlds, this struggle made a strong impression on me. I could see that the reformers were power-driven people, although they could express their urge to power only in terms of the higher needs of society. Carmine DiSapio, on the other hand, knew very little about the higher needs of society, but he knew for a fact that those Harvard kids wanted his job. And in the end they got it. In the name of the people, the upper classes took over politics in New York City. Then for a time a group of millionaires ran a city-state along the most advanced principles of political benevolence. In their view, any politician with a working-class accent was by definition corrupt.

THE LATE-LATE CAPITALIST

My experience has been that when the critical balance arrives between the established institutions and a new class with new demands, the institutions are not capable of defending themselves competently, or even of perceiving their own interests. They acquire an almost trained incapacity to know what to do. I went through a conflict of this kind years ago when I was working on the problem of traffic safety. It was a conflict that, owing to the entrenched obtuseness that afflicted the automobile manufacturers, eventually resulted in legislation imposing design regulations on their industry. It started in Albany in the 1950s, when I was secretary to Governor Harriman and served as chairman of a committee (which I regret to say was called The Governor's Traffic Safety Policy Coordinating Committee).

Traffic safety was a problem no one knew how to handle. Yet except for the instruments of modern warfare, the automobile has had the largest single impact on society of any product of technology. And in some estimates that William Haddon and I gave in lectures at Syracuse University in 1959, we showed that approximately one automobile in three which was manufactured in Detroit ended up with blood on it. So the system failed at a high and persistent rate.

Using a combination of epidemiological analyses, technological transfer, political science, and other things, we had the problem solved sometime around 1958. I'm speaking of a solution in the sense that the problems in theoretical physics were solved on paper before anybody ever built a nuclear reactor. (When the first fission took place at the University of Chicago in 1942, they thought it was enough of an event to open a bottle of Chianti. Nothing more, because of course it worked.)

So we knew what to do about the traffic problem. We knew that it had been wrongly defined as a problem in driver behavior. We had found that it must be approached from an epidemiological angle, that instead of trying to change driver behavior, which cannot be done, you must change the consequences of driver behavior, which can. The answer was to redesign the vehicles, redesign the highways, adapt a certain kind of elementary technology which had been used in airplanes for fifty years—and the first-generation solution was there.

Once we saw that, it had a thrilling inevitability; the analysis was so clear that nothing could prevent it from taking hold. The next step was to go out to Detroit with the good news. "We've got something wonderful for you!" we said. "We've solved the problem. We can show you why the system hasn't worked in the past, and we can show you what to do to make it work. A lot of engineering is required, but you're good at that kind of thing. You'll enjoy doing it, and you'll make money, because it doesn't cost much." Most of the first-order measures we suggested would actually lower the cost of automobiles, though ultimately there would be a cost-raising period. But the automobile companies couldn't follow us. They just didn't understand what we were saying.

Kenneth Galbraith would claim that the auto manufacturers have created the public taste and the market for what they supply. On the contrary, I believe that they mirror the market; they reflect what people want because they themselves want the same things. The reason they're so good is that they're so ordinary, if you don't mind my saying so. They really like the way a Plymouth sedan looks; that's the car they want, and their sense of what they want is what the public will want.

Though elites are always appalled by it, this principle is the basis of American culture. The elite was contemptuous of the crude and unaesthetic people who ran Hollywood in the 1930s, but looking back we find that it was the Golden Age of the American Screen. There's the story about Harry Cohn of Columbia Pictures, one of the crudest of them all, telling how he decided whether a movie was good or bad. If he began to squirm in his seat, he said, the movie wasn't going to make it. And Herman J. Mankiewicz, that brilliant, self-destructive screenwriter, said, "Imagine—the whole world wired to Harry Cohn's ass!" Yet Cohn was right in his way; when he began to squirm, people all over the world would leave the theater. The same with automobiles; what Detroit likes, the world will like.

What we found in Detroit was incomprehension. The manufacturers did not take in what we were saying—that automobiles can be designed so that you can have a crash and walk away from it. Their answer was, "People don't want cars that have crashes. People want cars that won't have crashes, and we're not about to sell them a car by telling them, 'When you have a crash in this car, you'll feel happy!' We sell cars that don't have crashes."

And when we said, "But you do have crashes!" they said, "That's the nut behind the wheel." They would not even consider the idea that a crash was a normal experience. There was a lot of magic in their creed: An "accident" was something you couldn't predict and couldn't do anything about. Yet the statistics said that one car in three would have blood on it before it was sent to the junkyard.

We fell back to recover, and returned to Detroit. "If you don't do this on your own," we said, "You know that the federal government will eventually make you do it." That's what happened to the railroads; it was safety as much as anything else which led to the ICC. We asked the auto executives: "Have you ever been to the ICC? You go in the building and come out a year older. Do you want that to happen to you? Do you want it to happen to us, for capitalism to take such a blow in our own country?" But they thought we were saying that we wanted it to happen.

So I went to Washington, where I wrote statements on traffic safety for John F. Kennedy in the 1960 campaign. I became assistant secretary for policy planning and brought Ralph Nader down to work on it. We thought that establishing some safety standards would take eight to ten years; it took four. But in the process, a bad fall for American capitalism! The sudden precipitation of a mood that was building up. The presumption of wrongdoing on the part of big business—a presumption which I think is now widespread. And the beginning of movements like Campaign GM and the demand for corporate responsibility.

THE LIMITS OF RESPONSIBILITY

The notion of corporate responsibility in a general sense is not difficult. Certainly capitalist organizations are accountable for the first-order and second-order effects of their work. The automobile companies are indeed responsible for the safety of their cars. Drug manufacturers are responsible for the safety of their compounds, and so forth. That's not hard to understand.

If you could keep the concept of corporate responsibility within these limits, the principle would be beneficial for business and for society. But when you begin placing demands on corporate systems that they cannot meet, the prospect is that the whole idea of accountability will expand to include all kinds of normative injunctions. It seems obvious that we're going to get more and more government regulation, which will make business less and less efficient.

There are other societies where the anticapitalist attitude is deeply ingrained, and the result is that they have never had capitalism. Look at what Paul Samuelson calls the miracle of Argentinian nongrowth: it was hard to mess up the economy of Argentina to the point where it achieved stagnation, but the Argentinians managed.

If the notion of corporate responsibility is pushed too far—if business is forced to become a normative instead of a utilitarian institution—there will be a politicalization of the business community, and a kind of elite ordering of priorities. When anyone declares that we've got to reorder priorities in this country, what he's aiming for is a situation where people do what he thinks is best, in contrast to a market situation. It's a fairly novel experience for me to be arguing on these lines, but I would say that the market has a lot more to do with the perpetuation of a democratic and libertarian society than you might think.

Schumpeter in his day, Milton Friedman in ours, have pointed out that the connection between capitalism and liberty is extraordinarily close. There are postcapitalist societies that are still more or less libertarian, but there are no precapitalist societies that are. None; not one!

Curiously, at any given time in the past fifty years most of the world's intellectuals have been committed to some form of tyranny or other. They have always proclaimed their commitment as the fearless adoption of a higher form of liberty, whereas in fact they have simply been advocating larger systems of concentration camps.

Writing at the end of the Depression, when things were not nearly what they ought to have been in this country, and certainly not what they are now, Schumpeter said:

> *Radicals may insist that the masses are crying for salvation from intolerable sufferings, and rattling their chains in darkness and despair, but of course there never was so much personal freedom of mind and body for all, never so much readiness to bear with and even to finance the mortal enemies of the leading class, never so much active sympathy with real and faked sufferings, never so much readiness to accept burdens, as there is in modern capitalist society. And whatever democracy there was outside of peasant communities developed historically in the wake of both modern and ancient capitalism.*

To conclude, I want to say to you that in the general assault on business values—and on the corporation, the primary institution of business management in this country—we may find ourselves closer to the taproots of a democratic society than we like to think. Whether we shall cut that root is the real question. The problem is that the people who are most responsible for the maintenance of this institution, who have perhaps the most interest in perpetuating it, are mute.

American capitalism is incapable of pleading its case with anybody. It has no intellectuals, saving a few men like Friedman, whom it doesn't understand. It has no periodicals. It has no publicists of any competence. It has a lot of people on the payroll, but they're no good. With our study of traffic problems we went to General Motors and said, "Please, this is in your interest," and General Motors couldn't follow us. And since corporations are behaving in much the same way today, I assume that over the next generation we will see a strong increase in the politicization of corporate affairs, an imposition of elite values, and probably a pronounced decline in economic vitality.

QUESTIONS AND ANSWERS

You've painted a gloomy picture of the future for American business. Do you see it as a reality? And if it does come to pass, is there any escape?

In the examinations that used to be given for the British Colonial Service, a young man would be asked, "Suppose you are a district officer near Kuala Lumpur in Malaya, and you're walking to a village 60 miles away. You're on your own, 30 miles into the jungle, cutting your way through, when suddenly you are struck in the forearm by a king cobra. You have a knife and matches; that's all. What do you do?" And the correct answer was that you die.

But I don't envision anything like that happening. I do think there is likely to be a diminished vitality in American capitalism. I think it will come at a time when we are at an optimal condition in the consumption of goods and services. So far, even in good times many Americans have been in want. But over the long term Americans are getting closer to the optimal point, in the sense of diminishing returns on increased consumption. More and more people have to watch their weight, and so does the society, as it were.

Therefore a certain slowing of that kind of growth is, I think, consistent with our interests. The thing that I am concerned about is the problem of employment. If American enterprise becomes less vital, we have the possibility of becoming a kind of a "rentier" society. We may begin living off investments and making a trade-off which I almost feel already: letting our unproductive industries and our unproductive workers go down the drain, importing the goods, and maintaining a large population in conditions of relative dependency, because it's just easier that way. Get your knitwear from Hong Kong, and keep people on welfare in Chicago, Manhattan, and South Carolina.

There's something the matter with a situation in which New York City has one person in six on welfare. It reflects this absence of economic vitality. It may also reflect a certain kind of economic populism that drives wages up to the point where people do become marginal, and we end up buying in Hong Kong.

But don't underestimate the capacity of entrepreneurs to adapt to a new business climate. The Bell System is, after all, a public utility. You've lived in different business climates at various times, and you've succeeded.

You gave some figures on the deterioration in confidence in some of our social institutions. And you also indicated that there may be some conflict between the values of, say, religious organizations and business corporations. But you didn't indicate where the obligations of the academic community which you represent are with respect to the criticism leveled at other institutions.

Let me say that when I contrasted religious with business institutions, I was simply contrasting a normative mode of organization with a utilitarian mode. In the two types people get ahead in

different ways, and they express aggression through different chan-
nels. For example, nobody ever wants to be Pope; he's always
willing to be Pope if elected.

Now, I said that intellectuals are always going to be opposed to
a capitalist society. In the last 30 to 40 years, the universities have
become places where intellectuals are. This wasn't true before that;
if you had called a Harvard professor an intellectual in 1935 he
might well have taken offense. Intellectuals were people who lived
in Greenwich Village and had mistresses. Harvard professors were
scholars, a very different thing. But now the academic community
is an intellectual community, and it will always be critical of
capitalism.

According to Schumpeter, the single most important fact about
capitalism is that as a society it is incapable of winning the loyalty
of the intellectual classes. He says it just doesn't happen, never
happens. And he wasn't referring to New York in 1970. He was
talking about life in Vienna after World War I, life in Berlin: he
was talking about the history of this phenomenon. He wrote in the
1940s about the capitalist process and how it produced an atmosphere of almost universal hostility to its own social order.

As for the press, which Schumpeter thought of as the intellectual
profession, let me read you an excerpt from an address given several years ago by a distinguished American television correspondent. Listen to him describing to a university audience what he
sees as his role and that of his colleagues in Washington:

"What the national media, and mainly television, have done is to
believe that their chief duty is to put before the nation its unfin-
ished business: pollution, the Vietnam war, discrimination, continuing violence, motor traffic, slums. The media have become the
nation's critics, and as critics no political administration, regardless
of how hard it tries, will satisfy them."

That's a "no win" situation. No matter what you do, you're not
going to satisfy us. We are your critics.

Remember that the correspondent does not represent an elee-
mosynary institution but a very efficient capitalist one. Capitalists
will do anything to make money; it's an old—and not unattractive
—capitalist tradition. From the political scientist's viewpoint one
of the great things about capitalism is that it diverts so much energy from the political system that politics does not become over-
loaded. The people who are scrambling around trying to make the
telephone system work, and trying to get a raise out of it, are not
shooting each other over who's going to be district leader in the
15th Assembly District South.

*In terms of the normative and utilitarian categories, it seems
to me that our business and many others once were normative. We used to tell the public what service it needed. Now
we're discovering we have to provide the service that the
public wants. And in a country which is becoming increasingly
service-oriented, aren't we going to have to become more
utilitarian, in order to survive?*

That's a complex statement worthy of John Kenneth Galbraith. I
would say, sure you tried to induce demand for something called
telephones. You told the public that telephoning is better than
shouting, better than writing, that all the fancy people in town
have a telephone, so why not you?

But basically you were providing a service which people really
did want, once they became aware of it. You didn't artificially
create their desire to call somebody up in another part of town.
Once it became possible, they wanted to. And the way you went
about selling telephones was very straightforward and utilitarian.

I remember a point that C. P. Snow made about the post office
system, and I'll apply it to the telephone system. In the early stages
of industrial development, a lot of clever people are around. There
are plenty of bright kids who haven't had very large opportunities.
They didn't go to Oxford or Columbia, and they're looking for a

job somewhere, and they find one in the post office. And they get in that job and they're smart; they make the post office run like crazy. I remember that in London just after the war, you could put a letter in a post box before 10 o'clock in the morning and it would be delivered before 4 o'clock in the afternoon. Today you can place a long-distance call before 10 o'clock in the morning and get it before 4 o'clock in the afternoon.

The smart fellows were in the post office because it was the best job they could get. But now in England if you're that smart, they spot it early and you don't go to work for the post office. You go to work in a system that rewards merit more quickly, and it's a more elitist system. I wouldn't be surprised if you in the Bell System were finding that people with such natural competence can get better jobs elsewhere. Let me put it this way: if the women's groups have anything to do with it, you're not going to be able to draw on an unlimited pool of married women to run your switchboards. The more mobile ones will get jobs that move them up to their levels of ability, which may be beyond your system right now. Am I making sense? A little bit of sense? All right, I'll settle for that.

SELECTED WRITINGS OF DANIEL P. MOYNIHAN

Coping: On the Practice of Government, Random House, New York, 1973.

Maximum Feasible Misunderstanding, Free Press, New York, 1969.

The Politics of a Guaranteed Income, Random House, 1973.

Toward a National Urban Policy (editor), Basic Books, New York, 1970.

POWER SHIFTS
IN AMERICAN
DEMOCRACY

HANS J. MORGENTHAU

*Born in Germany and educated at the Universities of Berlin,
Munich, and Frankfurt, Hans J. Morgenthau was a teacher of law
and a jurist in Frankfurt when Hitler rose to power. He left Germany in 1932 and came to the United States in 1937. Here he has
taught at the University of Chicago, Harvard, Northwestern, Columbia, Yale, the University of Kansas, and the City University of
New York. He has also served as a consultant to the State and
Defense Departments and as senior fellow of the Council on Foreign Relations. Morgenthau is now professor of political science at
the New School for Social Research in New York City.*

I WANT to discuss with you some of the basic problems of American democracy. One is the shift of power from the people to the government. Another is the shift within the government from the democratically responsible agencies to certain elites which are not controlled by democratic procedures.

Let me first give you a definition of a democracy, or at least of the ideal type of democracy. An ideal system of democratic government would make it possible for the electorate to choose among different people, and by doing so, to choose among different policies. If there were three candidates, A, B, and C, each candidate would represent a different philosophy, or at least a different policy. By choosing one over the other, you would be choosing not only a person, but also a program.

Applying this definition to current American politics, you realize right away the extent to which the actual practice of democracy differs from its ideal.

Take a backward look at the Presidential election of 1964, where the two candidates, Lyndon Johnson and Barry Goldwater, not only were quite different in personality, but also appeared to represent entirely different political philosophies and policies. But once Johnson was elected, he started to pursue the policies which his opponent had represented, at least in the foreign field. The people who had voted for Johnson because they liked his foreign policy found that in effect, he had turned into Goldwater. In this case there was a reversal of roles, with a man who stood for one philosophy and one policy during the campaign pursuing the policy of his opponent after the election.

In the campaign of 1968, on the other hand, the difference between the platforms of Hubert Humphrey and Richard Nixon was slim. This points again to a deficiency in our democratic processes. It is no longer primarily a question of philosophy and policy which is presented to the electorate, but of two personalities. It is a matter of taste, or of the way in which a particular candidate comes across on TV, which decides the issue. Certainly this is a considerable divergence from the ideal of a democratic system as I have defined it.

POWER TO REVOLT

Moving to a more specific issue, which bears directly upon the distribution of power between the people and the government, you find that a fundamental change has occurred in recent times. Formerly in the relations between the government and the people, there always existed the implicit threat of revolution. That is, if the policies of a government became unbearable for the people, they had the option of revolting against the government. Jefferson said that there ought to be a revolution in each generation. The American Revolution is a classic example: the policies of the British government became unbearable for the colonists, and they started shooting.

Throughout history, the possibility of a popular revolution against the government had ensured the essential equality of the people and the government. The people were not inferior to the government in military power; they had their knives and muskets, and they took them out from under their beds and went into the streets. The outcome was a matter of organization, of numbers, of leadership. For example, during the Napoleonic wars when the Spaniards revolted against the French army, they went into the streets and started attacking and killing Frenchmen. Since there were more Spaniards there than Frenchmen, and since the Spaniards had the better cause, they drove the Frenchmen out.

Today any government in a technologically advanced society has a quasi-monopoly of the modern technologies of communication, transportation, and warfare. So there is an extreme inequality in military power between the people and the government. Popular revolution has become impossible.

A little more than a century ago, one section of the American people found the policies of the federal government unbearable. They took to arms and fought the Civil War, because there still existed, 110 or so years ago, a rough equality between the people and the government in the implements of war. But when a revolt started less than 20 years ago in Little Rock, Arkansas, the presence of one division of American troops decided the issue; no shot was fired. Today it is inconceivable that one section of the American people could take arms against the federal government.

In times past, the threat of revolution was the most effective restraint upon the actions of the government. The government knew that if it consistently went too far, it would have to face the armed mass of its people. Today a government can do virtually what it wants to as long as it has the support of the armed forces and the bureaucracy. It is no accident that the last popular revolution occurred in a country which was a technologically backward one: Russia in 1917. Since then the revolts in technologically advanced nations have not been revolutions but coups d'etat. The armed forces, not the people, revolt against the government and either take it over or put somebody in whom they trust.

This is an example of a shift of power both away from the people and, within the government, away from the democratically elected representatives to an elite. The military elite is not democratically responsible; it has only one great advantage—that it is in the monopolistic possession of the organized instruments of violence. The Federalist Papers show that the Founding Fathers were mortally afraid of a standing army, exactly because they feared that a standing army would exert a political influence which could not be democratically controlled. In Great Britain they didn't dare to establish a permanent police force until the 1830s, because they were afraid that any organization which was practiced in violence would impair the democratic processes of government.

DECISION MAKING IN MODERN SOCIETY

There is a great paradox in the fact that the franchise is much broader today than it has ever been. Fifty years ago women were still prevented from voting, and until very recently certain minorities were handicapped in exercising their political rights. The poll tax was one instrument that prevented poor people of all races from voting. Not only have these restrictions been removed today, but young people from the ages of eighteen to twenty-one have been enfranchised. Yet the people have much less influence upon the processes of government than they had in the past.

Why is this so? I think the answer lies primarily in the nature of the issues with which a modern society is confronted.

One of the great issues at the beginning of this century, for example, was the question of labor unions. Should they be considered criminal conspiracies, as they had been regarded in common law, or should they be legitimized as organizations of workingmen pursuing common objectives? The issue was simple, and it was easy for the man in the street to decide where he stood.

Other labor problems in the early 1900s concerned child labor and the working hours of women. The Supreme Court declared unconstitutional all state laws which prohibited child labor and limited women's working hours; it said this was an unconstitutional interference in the freedom of contract. Again the issues were simple, and the man in the street could take a position according to his prejudices, emotions, philosophy, and interests. He could support the state which tried to reform labor relations, or he could support the Supreme Court when it declared the legislation unconstitutional.

Today, controversy over labor relations involves issues infinitely more complex. The man in the street may say to hell with unions or he may be in favor of them. But neither he nor the expert has any simple answers to questions about how to ensure democracy within unions, or how to control the financial activities of unions, or how to protect the individual union member against unethical financial practices.

Again, consider the issue of race relations, which 110 years ago was simply the issue of slavery versus emancipation. The man in the street had a simple answer on the basis of his personal inclinations and interests. But the topic of race relations today is surrounded with enormous complexity. Take the problems of race relations in the area of elementary and secondary schools. These problems defy any kind of clear-cut, manageable answer even by experts. The other day I listened to a discussion by leading educators on schools in the inner city, and it was obvious from the clichés they used that they had no answers. Anybody can see that there are problems, but nobody can find answers.

The same is true with military problems. Just before World War II Congress decided, with one vote to spare, to continue the draft. The question was simple and so was the answer. But today the government has to make decisions on nuclear weaponry. Should there be a continuous quantitative and qualitative arms race with the Soviet Union? Should there be a defensive system to protect the cities, or should there be missile installations, or both? The man in the street can't even understand the issues, let alone give answers.

And so the electorate has a general feeling of helplessness. The issues of today are not intelligible to the average voter, and more important, they do not appear manageable to the average voter. Even if voters were to understand the issue, for instance, with regard to race relations, they haven't got an answer in practical operational terms. All those experiences in different fields lead to one conclusion: Leave it to the experts, leave it to the government. If personal interests are involved, the individual may become active. Otherwise, when the public at large is involved, when the great issues of state are decided, leave them to the government, leave them to the experts. I can't remember how often I was told, when I debated the issue of the Vietnam war six or seven years ago: "Who are you to put your judgment against the judgment of the President? What do you know that the President doesn't know?" Which is another way of saying, "Leave it to him, he knows best. You keep your mouth shut." Which in retrospect I think might have been wise, except that it would have violated what I regard as a moral requirement of democratic citizenship.

The "leave it to George" argument is, of course, essentially non-democratic. If everybody followed this advice, the government would decide what to do, and the people would follow, and democratic controls would disappear.

POWER IN CONGRESS

Not only does the electorate feel helpless in our technologically advanced society, but the people's elected representatives in Congress are not qualified to pass judgment on some of the technological issues at stake. Take a look sometime at the Congressional Record and see in what cavalier fashion Congress disposes of the military budget. I'm not criticizing Congress; nobody who doesn't have an enormous technical apparatus at his disposal is capable of understanding that budget. The military authorities tell Congress that $83 billion is the minimum necessary to protect the United States. Who in Congress is going to get up and say, "You Joint Chiefs of Staff are wrong; $69 billion will do"? Nobody has the technical knowledge to make such a statement. Congress will ritualistically cut $1 or $2 billion from the budgetary request, just in order to convince itself and the folks back home that it is doing its job. But as a matter of fact, nobody in Congress understands the complexities of the military issues involved in the budget.

Besides the difficulty of comprehending the issues in a modern democracy, structural factors inherent in our form of government limit the power of Congress to govern. Take the issue of war-making powers. According to the Constitution, it is for Congress to declare war. But certainly neither the Korean war nor the Vietnam war was declared by Congress; both were decided upon by the executive branch. A great many members of Congress, both liberals and conservatives, have looked for means to limit the powers of the President in this respect.

We are confronted here with an existential limit upon democratic control. I should say that the conflict between the President and Congress concerning the determination of American foreign policy goes back to the beginnings of the republic. It is largely the result of the vagueness of the Constitution. That document assigns certain prerogatives to the President: representation abroad, for instance, and reception of ambassadors. It reserves other prerogatives to the Congress at large: peace and war. Others again to the Senate: ratification of treaties, the appointment of ambassadors. But it says nowhere who is ultimately responsible for the determination of American foreign policy.

And so, as pointed out by one of the most competent recent commentators on the Constitution, Edward S. Corwin of Princeton University, the constitutional provisions concerning foreign policy are a standing invitation for conflict between the executive and the legislative branches. Congress can jeopardize a President's foreign policy, as the Senate did Wilson's League of Nations policy by refusing to ratify the Treaty of Versailles. It can delay action on foreign policy. It can hamstring a President's policy. But even if it defies the President, it cannot substitute a foreign policy of its own for the President's.

So the executive branch has a natural superiority here, a superiority which is not limited to foreign policy. It is not strictly accurate to define democracy as government by the people, of the people, for the people. It cannot be government by the people, because the people at large, you and I, cannot govern. In theory what we can do—and here I come back to the point I started with —what we can do ideally is to elect individuals who are committed to certain policies. And if we are satisfied with those elected officials and their policies, we can reelect them. And if we are dissatisfied we can elect somebody else more competent, or somebody committed to a different policy; but we can't govern ourselves. So you see, government has a natural superiority which democratic rhetoric has tended to obscure.

POWER OF THE MAJORITY

Let me make one more point concerning the crisis of democracy today: a point about the critical relationship between majority rule and minority rights. Democracy is obviously ruled by the majority. The majority decides, it elects, and by electing, it at least believes that it decides upon policies. But if there were nothing else to democracy except majority rule, the majority would keep itself in power indefinitely. This is what has happened in totalitarian countries; typically a minority has transformed itself into a majority by monopolistic exploitation of the means of communication, transportation, and warfare.

An essential condition for democracy is that the minority of today have a chance to become the majority tomorrow. The distribution of power between majority and minority must not be fixed once and for all.

This is one of the most difficult achievements of a democratic order. We all have a tendency to believe that our convictions, our interests, our politics are a reflection of the objective laws of the universe. What I want, what I am interested in, I think everybody ought to want and be interested in. The group that is in the majority needs enormous moral restraint to admit that perhaps the minority also has a point—that at least the minority should have a chance to make its point, and a chance to become the majority.

I have always been impressed with Oliver Cromwell's appeal to a delegation of Scotch Presbyterians. He said: "I beseech you, by the bowels of Christ, deem it possible that you may be mistaken." He stated the most difficult moral achievement of an individual and of a community. But this moral restraint—this conviction that while I am right and ought to prevail, the other side ought to have a chance to prevail too—is necessary for the survival of democracy.

Consider the history of democratic government, especially in Anglo-Saxon countries, from the Magna Charta onwards through the English and American Revolutions. Democratic processes originated in a power struggle between the king and first the nobles, then the people at large. But the consummation of this quantitative extension of political activity did not occur until our century. Examples that I have already mentioned are women's suffrage, which is a relatively recent phenomenon, and the extension of the vote to young people between eighteen and twenty-one.

There has been a gradual development from the thirteenth century onwards, in which ever larger groups of people did not govern themselves, but put limits upon the powers of the government. In the American Constitution the Founding Fathers showed their concern to circumscribe the government's authority. The real issue was not to allow the people to govern themselves, which is a technical impossibility. Rather, it was to give the populace *influence* upon the government. The people can select the officials who govern them, but they can't govern themselves. So the development of democratic rule has been the development of restraints upon the powers of the government.

The very fact that we have periodic elections puts limits upon the government authority. The people who govern us want to be reelected, and if for constitutional reasons they can't stand for reelection, they want their party to stay in power. So the fact that the tenure of the government depends upon the electoral process exerts a direct influence upon government behavior.

Another conception of democracy, which developed from the French Revolution and which prevailed in France up to the rise of de Gaulle, is that democracy means the rule of the majority. That is, the decisions of the majority of the Chamber of Deputies in Paris became the law. This approach to democracy led to semianarchy because of the natural divisions of interest, power, and personalities in a large popular assembly. The successive breakdown of different French Republics has resulted in the Fifth Republic, which is a kind of semi-authoritarian, semi-parliamentary, semi-presidential system.

In this country we have never taken the position that the rule of the majority is the ultimate point of reference for government action. Look at the Supreme Court, which is not democratically responsible to the electorate. The Court can overturn acts of Congress, as well as measures taken by the executive branch, in the name of what the nineteenth century called the "higher law." By its very nature the higher law is exempt from democratic determination. The Founding Fathers believed that certain objective principles are self-evident, representing a kind of natural law which evolves from the nature of things and which no majority is capable of overturning. If a majority tries to violate them, the Supreme Court will see to it that they are observed.

Another "undemocratic" device which can overturn the decision of the majority is the Presidential veto. In short, the American system of government, which is a democratic system, is not necessarily a majoritarian system. It is much more complex, and consequently much more successful, than majoritarian systems like the French Republics.

Unfortunately, this country's classic Anglo-Saxon concept of democratic government has recently been yielding to the majoritarian principle. Our government is more majoritarian now than it was 200 or 100 or even 50 years ago. To a large extent the crisis of democratic government today is the result of this watering down of the principles of American democracy in favor of majoritarian rule. Here, I believe, is the grave danger for American democracy.

There is a popular notion that totalitarianism is the result of concentrating power in the hands of the government. The idea is that the accumulation of power leads to a tyranny in which the government can act without constitutional restraints. Yet when we look at the development of German and Italian fascism, we find that it did not result from the strength of the central government but from its weakness. Men want to be free—this is one impulse, one aspiration they have; but they also want to be governed. When we speak of "law and order" as a prerequisite for effective government, we are dealing with the second aspiration.

The democratic governments in Italy and Germany which preceded the takeovers by fascism were unable to govern effectively. It was the disorder, the semianarchy which arose in those countries that led people to sacrifice their freedom in order to get competent government. The saying that Mussolini made the trains run on time is one expression of the need to have a modicum of order even at the expense of freedom.

The first thing a fascist government does is to artificially create a majority that will support it forever. No minority which could challenge the majority is allowed to exist. The interplay of the majority of today with the minority which may become the majority tomorrow is the very essence of the democratic process. What fascism does is to abolish this dynamic relationship.

The basis of a working democracy is a kind of relativism about where truth and virtue reside. The majority claims them for itself, but there is always the assumption that perhaps the minority may also have a slice of truth and that the majority may not have a monopoly on virtue. In a totalitarian country people are not allowed to think that the government can be mistaken. Whoever dissents is either a traitor or a madman. There is a grim logic in the Russian practice of sending political dissenters to insane asylums.

The point I want to make is that democracy is an extremely difficult form of government to manage successfully. I think it is to the credit of this country that for almost 200 years it has been able to make democracy work. Let us beware of the pitfalls of democratic government, so that we can solve the critical problems which democracy faces today.

THE NEW FEUDALISM: Power in Organizations

I have described the shift in military power from the people to the government that has made popular revolution impossible. I have also discussed the enormous complexity of the issues that the electorate and the Congress must decide today. Now let me turn to another factor which is intimately connected with the complexity of issues: the huge power of organizations, public and private.

In the United States 100 or 150 years ago, the power of the government was far superior to the power of private organizations. Today there are establishments such as General Motors and U.S. Steel—I shall not mention any mass communication corporations —that operate in a sense as private governments. Their decisions on wages, working conditions, production, and technological changes significantly affect the whole nation, not just their own members. When U.S. Steel increases prices, it is an economic and political fact of paramount importance. And not even under price and wage controls can a public government control the decisions of private governments.

What we have here is a kind of new feudalism. These concentrations of private power are unprecedented in scope and largely exempt from control by the public government. Since the 1880s the public government has tried to control the private governments through regulatory commissions, and we all know what has happened: the private governments have come to control the regulatory commissions. The Interstate Commerce Commission is the first and classic example of the reversal of functions. Before the railroads were nationalized, the ICC had become a kind of executive committee of the railroad companies.

Although in relation to the people the government is more powerful than ever before, compared with the concentrations of private power it is much less powerful. So the concentration of government power relative to the people has not resulted in greater total power of government. The idea of resorting to wage and price controls shows the government's desperation in the face of unemployment, inflation, and a recalcitrant pluralism of private powers.

In a sense, the federal government is in the position of the medieval king confronting his feudal lords. He could not operate without them, especially when it came to military matters, to war. And he had to pay them—in honors, in political power, in lands, in money—to get their support. Similarly, in what is now called the military-industrial complex the public powers of the federal government are provided by private corporations. Without their aid the government could not perform its functions.

So the sources of power in private organizations are dual. First, it is impossible for the government to control these organizations in a democratic society. Second, their support is indispensable to the government. When Lockheed went broke, it was logical for the government to appropriate $250 million to bail it out. For Lockheed is not a private organization which can go out of business without harming the public interest; it is a private government whose services are vital to the public government.

There is a tendency for the public agencies—Congress, the Supreme Court, the President, and the executive branch of the government—to go through the motions of performing their constitutional and traditional functions, while the real decisions are made elsewhere, without any democratic control. They are made by U.S. Steel, by General Motors, by the intertwined personnel of the military-oriented industries and the Pentagon.

The political apathy which is widespread in the United States is nourished by this situation. The man in the street asks, "What difference does it make who I vote for, or whether I vote at all?"

POLICY AND PUBLIC OPINION

Finally, there is another weakness in contemporary democratic government: a misunderstanding about the relationship between the government and what we call public opinion. Obviously a democratic government must govern with the consent of the people. That is, there must be a certain harmony between the policies of the government and the preferences of the people at large.

How can that harmony be established? In a totalitarian society it is based on terror. The government uses its monopoly of the mass media to brainwash the people at large, and uses its military power to get rid of the recalcitrant minority. It thus creates an artificial consensus by which it governs. But in a democracy the consensus is much more difficult to establish, especially when the government fears to govern effectively.

Let me give you an example. When John Foster Dulles was Secretary of State, a breakdown of public opinion was prepared for him every Monday morning. It dealt with the basic issues which he had to decide during the week and was supposed to show him how far he could go while retaining public support. This procedure has been followed by a succession of administrations. It assumes that public opinion precedes government policy, that all of us walk around with a set of convictions about the basic issues of government. If a pollster asks you about policy on Berlin—should the government do this, that, or the other—you're supposed to give an expert opinion. Ten years or so ago when the Berlin issue was at its height, those questions were in the polls, and the answers certainly had some influence upon government policy. Yet one poll asked a few factual questions, and it came out that around one-third of the people who had firm opinions about policy on Berlin didn't know that Berlin was surrounded by Communist territory.

Political folklore assumes that everybody has opinions about public issues. The myth is that politicians should collect those opinions and classify them. Then government will know what public opinion is, and what policies to follow. But this is pure fiction. You and I have opinions about most issues not because we have made an independent investigation, or because we have thought deeply about them, but because we have read or heard opinions that we accepted. In other words, we have digested the opinions of people in whose judgment we have confidence.

In a democracy public opinion is partly, or perhaps predominantly, the result of the policies of the government. In the early fifties, for example, polls were taken continuously to measure people's attitudes toward the recognition of Communist China. There were always substantial majorities against it. In the fall of 1956 President Eisenhower intimated in a press conference that perhaps under certain conditions we might pursue a two-China policy. The next public opinion poll showed a majority in favor of a two-China policy. Eisenhower didn't follow the matter up, and public opinion reverted to its previous mold. Four years ago, the polls showed the same overwhelming support for the traditional policy of no relations, no recognition. Yet today public opinion decisively approves the government's two-China policy. So the tendency of government officials to embark only upon policies which are endorsed by the public leads to an emasculation of public policy. A courageous government, an audacious government, creates public opinion on behalf of the policies it wants to pursue.

In summary, one of the most serious symptoms of the crisis of modern democracy is the fear of the government to govern. And one of the greatest dangers for democratic processes arises not in a powerful government but in a weak one that retreats from leadership. For the people will accept any replacement, democratic or undemocratic, that accepts the obligation to govern.

THE POWER OF CHOICE

I have said that people are tempted to become apathetic about public issues because those issues appear to be unintelligible and unmanageable. In my view, there is a misunderstanding here about the nature of the issues. It is true that the ABMs, to take one example, confront us with highly complex technological issues which only technicians and scientists are able to understand.

But those issues, when they appear for public discussion and public decision, are political rather than technological. And insofar as the choices are political, you and I or any technological illiterate has the ability to apply common sense and arrive at a conclusion. I know hardly anything about radar and electronic systems, but I can understand the alternatives confronting us in the proposal to establish either an area ABM system for population and industrial centers, or a pinpoint system for the protection of missile sites. I can grasp the political and military aspects of the choices and make up my mind accordingly.

And so it is with most, if not all, of the great issues of the day. They may have a technological base, but they are essentially political. And in political judgment the technologist has no advantage over you or me. So I would suggest that the people and their elected representatives take their courage into their hands. They need not be frightened by the esoteric character of modern technology if they look at the issues not as technological but as political ones. These issues are accessible to all of us, and their resolution depends on our good judgment, not on the omniscience of the experts.

SELECTED WRITINGS OF HANS J. MORGENTHAU

"Decline of Democratic Government" (in "This Fractured Democracy: A Special Sixtieth Anniversary Supplement"), *The New Republic*, Nov. 9, 1974.

In Defense of the National Interest: A Critical Examination of American Foreign Policy, Knopf, New York, 1951.

A New Foreign Policy for the United States, Praeger, New York, 1969. (Published for the Council on Foreign Relations.)

Politics among Nations: The Struggle for Power and Peace, 5th ed., Knopf, 1973.

Politics in the Twentieth Century (3 vols.), University of Chicago Press, 1962.

The Purpose of American Politics, Knopf, 1960.

Truth and Power: Essays of a Decade, 1960–70, Praeger, 1969.

AMERICANS
AND
THEIR CITIES

ॐ

IRVING KRISTOL

Irving Kristol, a native New Yorker and a graduate of City College, has been a writer, editor, and publisher in New York City for more than thirty years. From 1947 to 1969 he was editor of several magazines and executive vice-president of the publishing house, Basic Books. In 1969 he became Henry R. Luce Professor of Urban Values at New York University.

Together with Nathan Glazer he is co-editor of The Public Interest, *a magazine founded ten years ago by Kristol and Daniel Bell to promote the rational analysis of public issues. Kristol is a member of the National Council in the Humanities, the Council on Foreign Relations, and the American Academy of Arts and Sciences.*

I T'S my impression that people no longer get so excited about the urban crisis as they did four or five years ago. One hears less talk about it—especially from politicians, who are pretty good weathervanes. And I suspect the reason is that there has been so much talk in the past, so much money spent, so many different programs devised and launched, and so little accomplished. Obviously with so little real change in our cities after so much hoopla there's bound to be a drop in morale. This sets some people to wondering why. But it sets most people to deciding simply that they're more interested in another question. Usually in politics, as in mathematics, when a field becomes terribly difficult, politicians just move out of it. Mathematicians don't spend all their time on tough problems—the myth may be that they do, but in fact they don't. They just decide they'll go into a field where the problems are easier. Well, politics and social problems are not so very different. When the problem is intractable for any length of time, ordinary people get bored with it, and shift their attention to something they think they can cope with. Today we hear much more about reform of our political institutions than we do about the urban crisis. And neither our cities nor our political institutions are particularly different from what they were five or six or seven years ago.

Still, it is interesting to ask why all this talk and all this expenditure and all these programs had so little apparent effect. Do we have anything to learn from our experience with the urban crisis?

If you look in retrospect at this crisis, and look at all the programs that were launched to "solve" it, you see that there wasn't just one urban crisis. There were at least three, possibly ten or more. But for the purposes of this session, we will say there were three. The three urban crises were crises of three different groups. Each group looked at the city from its own perspective, experienced the city and its problems in its own way, and demanded that certain things be done to help or alleviate its conditions. Unfortunately, there is no way of reconciling the things that had to be done from the three perspectives. Since the three groups really wanted very different things, the programs that emerged from listening to these groups resulted in contradictory and conflicting programs. We thought there was one urban crisis. We thought we could locate discrete urban problems and solve them. But that's not the way urban problems are. Urban problems are people's problems. You don't solve them the way you solve mathematical questions. Urban problems usually involve conflicts of interests and conflicts of values. You either ignore them or establish some form of accommodation between the conflicting groups. Usually these accommodations are never entirely satisfactory to any one group.

What are the three groups I have in mind? The first group, which is not all that important in most American cities but happens to be terribly important in New York, is what we can call the patrician class. This class of pretty rich people wants New York City to be a more urbane city, a nicer city. They want New York to be like London. They want New York to be clean; have less crime; be more gracious; have more theaters, prettier buildings, and so on. A city fit for wealthy people. Patricians are inevitably very concerned with the environmentalist movement, because they are so deeply concerned with the environment in which they live. These are the people who helped build Lincoln Center, who support the Metropolitan Opera, and who contribute a great deal to New York City. They are very important, not simply because they're rich, though that's important, but rather because of their influence on the media. New York City is the media capital of the nation. The patrician class are the people who run your TV stations, put out all your magazines, run your book publishing houses, run the most important newspaper in the United States, *The New York Times*. These people's attitudes and prejudices are broadcast not only to the citizens of New York but to the whole world. Therefore they can impose their views far beyond the economic or political power they have, for their power comes more from their occupational position than from their money.

The patrician group is in conflict with the other two major groups in our city: one is the inner-city blacks and nonwhites (the poor people), and the other is the white working and middle classes. The working and middle classes are not found in Manhattan, where most patricians live. They reside primarily in Brooklyn, Queens, the Bronx, and to some degree, Staten Island.

The first conflict between the patricians and the other classes was over urban renewal. The patricians wanted urban renewal. "Let's restore downtown. Make it vital. Make it vibrant. Make it pretty. Bring customers back to the stores. Bring theatergoers back to the theaters," etc., etc. And urban renewal was the answer. Please remember that urban renewal was the first big government program to solve the urban crisis in the late forties and the early fifties. It looked great on paper. After it got going, people discovered that urban renewal was to the advantage of the patrician class and to the considerable disadvantage of other classes. For example, the poor blacks in the inner city found themselves being removed from one neighborhood after another as a result of these patrician efforts to save the city. So urban renewal, after having been hailed, praised, and enthusiastically acclaimed, quickly ground to a halt. There was great opposition from the nonpatrician elements in the city, who did not gain all that much from urban renewal and were immediately hurt.

One can find other conflicts, too. Although the patrician class, particularly in New York City, is on the whole a compassionate, liberal class, it creates conflicts. For example, these people don't really like seeing factories in the city. Factories are dirty. Their dirt pollutes the atmosphere. They're not particularly good for neighborhoods. They don't fit in with the patrician vision of the city. But factories are necessary in this city to create jobs for unskilled labor. One of the big problems of the poor people is the fact that after World War II many factory jobs moved out of the city into the suburbs, small towns, and smaller cities of America. Unquestionably this shift hurt the city's poor whites and poor blacks. It didn't really affect the patrician class one way or another. Talk with people along the Upper East Side who are liberal and are very much interested in civic affairs: they really *don't* think the garment center is a marvelous thing to have in New York City. It's crowded; it's noisy; it's dirty; it clutters up the streets, ties up traffic. They really can't get interested in the problems of the garment center. They really don't care that the garment center creates jobs for unskilled labor. They want a clean city. The patricians are at the forefront of the environmental or ecological movement. I predict that in the next five years or so there will be a head-on collision with the poorer people in New York City on this issue.

The patrician class has been successful so far in preventing construction of a fourth airport in the New York metropolitan area, largely because the media backed them. The media will usually back them . . . it's their media. But the fact is that something like 30,000 jobs hang on that fourth airport. The patrician class doesn't need the jobs. It may not even need a fourth airport, but there are a lot of people in the city who do need those jobs. The pressure for that fourth airport will build up again. At some point it will occur to a leader, either black or white, probably a leader in a trade union movement, that the airport is a good idea. In addition to the airport, I predict that we'll see another donnybrook with regard to Con Edison plants. The patrician class does not want Con Edison to build its plants within this city. Yet Con Edison is a pretty good employer. It offers good jobs. But if Con Edison has to build its plants a hundred miles away and pipe all the power into the city, those jobs will go with it.

In its ideas about what the urban crisis is and what needs to be done for the city, the patrician class comes into conflict with the non-rich, the non-well-to-do, whether black or white. The patrician class believes in school integration. Yet it sends its kids to private schools. On the whole, the patrician class has also been very compassionate about criminals. Most patricians go to psychiatrists, and they have a kind of psychiatric viewpoint on the world. They really believe that criminals are sick, and that with the right treatment everything will be all right. But then this class does not suffer from crime the way the other classes do. Patricians lead relatively sheltered and well-protected lives.

Look at the latest drug law in New York. Who was for it and who was against it? It's simple. I mean, the patrician class was against it, and everyone else was for it. Blacks, whites, Puerto Ricans were for it. Not the patrician class. Not *The New York Times,* CBS, NBC, *Time, Newsweek,* and the people on Wall Street. They thought it was brutal, severe, inhumane. It conflicted with their image of what a good society is like.

The patrician class also clashes with the white working class and the white middle class in the area of housing integration. This area involves not only the integration of races but also the integration of classes. And in America the integration of economic classes has always been infinitely more difficult than the integration of races. Getting rich people to live in the same building or even the same block with poor people is much harder than getting white to live with black or black to live with white.

Here again, patricians are not particularly affected. They are integrating other parts of the city. It's ridiculous to think of integrating Fifth Avenue; how do you go about it? Still, integration is an issue which patricians have imposed upon the city. But I suspect there'll be very few future efforts made in housing integration, or for that matter, school integration.

Basically, the kinds of policies that are agreeable to the patrician class make the white working class and the white middle class very nervous. It disturbs their neighborhoods, and neighborhoods mean a great deal to these people. Usually they have all their savings invested in their homes. They intend to live there the rest of their lives, or at least until they retire. Start making them insecure about their neighborhoods, and they become terribly frustrated, angry, and upset . . . and just move out of the city.

The patrician class in the city, though very liberal, also finds itself in conflict with the black community, particularly with poor blacks. The black community in our city has a basic and ineradicable historical problem. Namely, it is in the position of a new immigrant group, though it is in fact one of the oldest American groups we have. Blacks are now being asked, as it were, to go through the experience of new immigrants. This makes them resentful, and no wonder. Economic opportunity for poor people means jobs for relatively unskilled labor. Largely, it means factory work. New York at the moment is delighted to get new offices. New offices, however, don't solve the problems of the ghetto. The young black male in particular is not interested in, or good at, office work. This also applies to the young poor white male in certain sections of the city. He doesn't want to spend his time pushing paper around in an office. He wants to be working outdoors, or he wants to be working in a factory with other men, in a masculine milieu.

How do you encourage the construction of new factories in the city? It's very difficult. Our patrician class is not especially interested in new factories built or located within the city. So now you have the basic problem of choice, and there are two choices open to poor blacks and Puerto Ricans in the inner city. Either they get help, or they get out. Both choices have their problems. My own view, and I couldn't possibly prove that it's the right view, is that the thing to do is to help them get out. But whichever view you take, you have to be consistent in it, and develop a set of policies for it.

Now, welfare is not such a policy. It doesn't solve any problems. All it does is create a large dependent population in the city. If the patricians are serious about revitalizing the ghetto, or revitalizing black and Puerto Rican neighborhoods in this city, they have to bring industry into those areas. But industry doesn't like to go there. Communications and transportation are very difficult. My own view is that it probably won't work. The more sensible thing to do is to take all that welfare money and buy an automobile for every single poor family in the city: black, white, or Puerto Rican. Let them cope with the problem of finding jobs. They'll do much better by being able to commute to the suburbs from New York than we are likely to do in bringing jobs into the city. But you're not going to get that kind of answer to the problem. It creates air pollution, more crowding on roads, etc., etc., etc.

So you have three groups, all of whom are upset about the way life is going in the city. It is clear that these three groups—the well-to-do, the white working class and middle class, and the minority groups in the inner city—have different perspectives on the city. Sometimes they themselves are terribly confused about the matter; they don't understand the need for choice. But each group is experiencing the urban crisis in its own way. Pity the poor politicians who try to solve everything in a way satisfactory to all. They can get into such extraordinary muddles that they don't even know they're in a muddle. A wonderful example is found in New York City today on the questions of community control of schools and school busing for integration. At the moment we are committed officially to both.

It makes some sense to say that parents and their communities should control the schools so as to control their children's education. It makes some sense to say that we want to bus white and black children for the purposes of integration. But it makes no sense to say that we're going to have community control, and then take children out of their community schools and bus them to other schools. The point of community control is to have control over your children's education. The point of busing is integration. The two goals happen to be incompatible. You cannot have community control with busing; you end up with one community controlling other people's children. Nevertheless, both are the official policies of New York City today.

This gives us a clue to government's reaction whenever it is faced with groups that have conflicting interests, conflicting values, conflicting perspectives on the future. Government does not have the power to say, "We're going to choose the perspective of one group and sacrifice all the rest to that group." What government will do is precisely what government does do, what government has done. As he listens to their competing and incompatible demands, the politician says to the three groups, "All right, we've got a program for each of you." And he develops a whole set of programs, each one satisfying one group and all of them canceling each other out. For example, is it the policy of the federal government to help blacks escape from the inner city, or to help blacks improve their conditions in the inner city? No way of finding out. There are programs for both. There are programs encouraging blacks to stay in the city; there are programs encouraging blacks to leave the city; programs encouraging whites to stay in the city; programs encouraging whites to leave the city.

There are also programs for the patricians. The best example of a patrician urban program is rapid transit. Subways are being built in cities such as Washington, D.C., and Los Angeles even though every economist who has studied the subject says they should not be built. It is going to be fearfully expensive. And it's not going to work, simply because the population is widely dispersed. Rapid transit works when a city is like a wheel, with a lot of people living inside the rim or along its spokes and commuting to and from the hub. But that's not the population structure of Los Angeles. In Los Angeles people don't go to the center very much. No one lives there and only a few people go there to work in offices. A fixed subway system is no use to them. Whichever subway they take, they'll have to end up walking a mile. And they won't. They'll end up using their automobiles.

I predict that the same thing will be true in San Francisco with the new BART system. The same is certainly going to be true in Washington, since commuting by automobile is more convenient than by a public transit system. The average work trip in the United States today takes twenty minutes, and people who live in Washington usually take twenty minutes. Even if they live in the suburbs it rarely takes more than half an hour to get to work. These people are not going to give up the conveniences of their automobile in order to get on a subway which will let them off four, five, or eight blocks away from their destination.

Rapid transit is nevertheless a patrician vision of the city. The patricians themselves don't use public transportation very much, but they're in favor of getting everyone else's automobiles off the streets and having everyone else use public transportation. They are eager to make public transportation as elegant and pleasant as possible to attract people. I don't know any serious student of rapid transit who would agree that the system, say in Los Angeles, makes any sense. Yet it surely will be built to satisfy the media, which maintain that rapid transit is a good thing.

But what is fortunate in American society is that where government policies fail, or where they don't work as well as expected, it doesn't always matter that much. The thing about an open society like the United States is that people solve their own problems over a period of time. What form will the solution take? I don't know. I don't know whether the blacks in the inner city will decide to stay or leave. I suspect they're going to leave. If they do decide to leave, they'll figure out ways to leave without government programs. In fact, many of them are now doing that very successfully.

We have become accustomed to thinking that if government doesn't do it, nothing will happen. But a lot of things are always happening. This is a mobile, dynamic country. People are moving, changing, all the time. Things do happen, sometimes even when government pays no attention.

If you've read John Steinbeck's *Grapes of Wrath,* you remember the tremendous problem of the migrant farm population in the late thirties. No one at that time thought in terms of a government program. During the Depression, government didn't have any money. But if the money had been available, certainly there would have been a government program. The odd thing was that by 1950 the Oakies had vanished. Where did they go? No research has been done on it. We only research our failures, not our successes. Yet you can learn more from researching successes. It's important to know why you succeeded; you may never know why you failed. It takes years and years to realize what went wrong and why. It's easier to see why you're succeeding. Here were the Oakies, a large, sick, illiterate class—not only functionally illiterate, but literally illiterate. Twelve years later they were suddenly gone, and to this day no one knows exactly where. What happened was that American society somehow absorbed them. Some of them are rich now: in California they run the valleys which grow grapes, radishes, and things like that. Problematic areas will, over a period of time, get swallowed up because people who are given the chance are usually pretty good at coping with their own problems.

There are other instances. You may have noticed from old Jean Harlow movies, and even early Marilyn Monroe films, that there was something in all American communities called "the other side of the tracks." The other side of the tracks was not a metaphor; it literally existed. Through most American towns there ran a railroad. Decent people, self-respecting folks, lived on one side of the tracks. On the other side of the tracks lived all the poor people. They were the ones who occupied shanties, who got drunk, who had illegitimate children. You couldn't get them to hold a job. In 1939 there was a sociological study of an all-American town, by which I mean an all-WASP town, by Hollingshead, a Yale sociologist. He chose a typical small town, Quincy, Illinois, and found 25 percent of the people living in shanties, absolutely illiterate, hopeless, and helpless. They didn't have any drugs, but they were all alcoholics. All had prison records. Yet by 1950 they were all gone. Anyone can argue that without a college degree you can't get a job. But suddenly they were gone; a dynamic, expanding economy had somehow made room for them.

How did those people manage? What happened to them? I don't know. We don't study our successes, because the successes were not part of anyone's official policies. No one is claiming credit for them, so no one is studying them. Sociologists are always fearful that if they study successes, it'll make the rest of the society smug instead of compassionate and critical.

We've reached a condition that the Greeks used to call stasis; we can call it stalemate. But because we have reached that condition, it does not mean that things are going to get worse. They need not. They might get better. My own guess is that through the political process, the three groups within the city will work out some kind of accommodation, an accommodation more stable than any that government can impose. Their accommodation will probably allow people to help solve their own problems. In cities like New York, Chicago, and Philadelphia, any kind of improvement will come from the people themselves. I don't think you're going to get a radical, brilliant transformation of our cities into shiny new places.

New York will never be London. It never has been London. Americans don't want it to be London. But there's no reason why New York can't be a better place than it is. My own guess is that it will be. It could have been even today, if government hadn't become so deeply involved in a process it didn't understand and couldn't really control. Over the next ten years the situation in New York is probably going to get better, even though no one will admit it. No one will pay any attention to it, everyone will start losing interest in urban problems, and everyone will get interested in whatever is going wrong somewhere else in the society. I would say, however, that the loss of interest in the so-called urban crisis is probably the healthiest sign to have come out of our experience with the urban crisis of the past ten years.

QUESTIONS AND ANSWERS

Dr. Kristol, hasn't the so-called exodus of the middle class from the inner city created a continuously new environment for the city?

You must remember that this process has been going on from the very beginning of American cities. As America has expanded economically, a steady movement to the suburbs has taken place and poor people have moved into the cities. This is the history of American cities, and the reason why they are not like European cities. American cities are like processing depots; people come, stay, and then move on. New York has seen its middle class move out of the city from the very beginning. It has retained the middle class only because the city kept expanding its boundaries. The population of New York City today is 33 percent nonwhite. The population of Boston by 1880 was over 50 percent Irish, mostly new immigrants who had just come into the city. I'm sure people sat around Boston in 1880 and said, "My God, what are we going to do about this situation? The middle class is leaving the city. All these poor illiterate Irish are coming in. They drink a lot, they can't work. How are they ever going to cope?"

They said it about the Irish; they said it about the Jews. A book was written in 1905 by a distinguished social critic named Hunter, who ran a settlement house and knew a great deal about New York City affairs. In his chapter on the Jews, he proved that the Jews of New York City were doomed to a perpetual culture of poverty. He had all the official statistics and all the official statements from Jewish organizations to back him up. It was very plausible, but they didn't stay poor, and the Irish in Boston didn't, and the Italians everywhere didn't. They created the new middle class. It takes time. And one of our problems is a lack of patience.

People don't change. It takes two or three generations to effect a change. It's the children who usually move up. By the time a man or woman is twenty-one, even eighteen or even sixteen, he or she is fixed for life. You're not going to take someone who's seventeen or eighteen and a high school dropout and make an engineer out of him. There might be one or two such people, but you're not going to find a batch of them. That's not the way things work. However, if they become decent, solid, hardworking people with some money and a decent home, their children may move up a notch. Then their children's children may move up another notch. This is the way it has been. Upward social mobility is a slow process. If you look at it in terms of ten, fifteen years, whatever you see may deceive you. That is why Mr. Hunter, back in 1905, was deceived when he predicted that the Jews would be doomed not only to poverty but to criminality. He proved conclusively that the majority of the criminals in New York City were Jews. He also proved that this social crisis was going to perpetuate itself. It didn't, because the people decided they wouldn't allow it to.

Dr. Kristol: Correct me if I'm wrong. Are you saying that if we have an urban crisis, usually time takes care of it without our doing anything about it?

Well, time and people. Time itself sounds as though only time will take care of it, but the passing of time alone will not do it. I am making the assumption that the American people are not helpless, are not stupid, are not wards of the state. They know their own interests and can accomplish an awful lot. To say that the passage of time will take care of an urban crisis is misleading. It wasn't just the passage of time that transformed the Irish of Boston from a drunken underclass into a fairly prosperous, solidly established community. It was the fact that they did things during the time they had. I am assuming that the American people have not changed character to such a degree in the 1970s that they will stop trying to better their conditions, given the opportunities.

Who will replace the black on the lower-class rung?

I don't see the blacks or the Puerto Ricans being replaced by a new underclass. I think our immigration policy has taken care of that. We have about half a million immigrants coming into this country each year, but they are mainly skilled people who are not going to be an underclass. I think that over the next twenty years, as blacks, Mexicans, Puerto Ricans, and so on, move up the ladder, we won't have an underclass. Sweden doesn't have one. Britain doesn't have one, or it didn't until a few years ago. There is no need to have one. The society can function without one. It plays no indispensable role.

You said that the slums have disappeared from the American cities. How about Harlem?

I said they have disappeared from many American cities. They certainly have not disappeared from New York, Philadelphia, or Chicago. When you get into the smaller American towns, like Quincy, Illinois, you don't find slums. You may find poor neighborhoods, but a poor neighborhood is different from a slum. A slum is a place where people are self-destructive. A poor neighborhood is just a place where people don't have the money to make it a better neighborhood.

How do you explain families that are on welfare for three or four generations?

First of all, the statistics are highly questionable. You must remember that to have been on relief in the 1930s meant nothing. Everyone was on relief if he could get it. Statistics of people whose fathers or grandfathers were on relief are meaningless. Besides, there aren't that many families who have been on relief for two or three generations. These represent an oddity, because the welfare population is a mobile one. People move on welfare and off welfare. It is true that among poor people there is a greater incidence of going on welfare at some time or another. What do poor people do if they get sick? They go on welfare for a while until they get well; then they move off. The number of families which have been on welfare for long periods of time is a very small proportion of the whole. Those figures have been misinterpreted and inflated.

Do you see a chance of the government ever refraining from spending money on ineffectual programs?

No. The government will continue to spend money on ineffectual programs. There are limits to how much we can foresee the consequences of any particular program. When the FHA was formed to help people buy their homes, no one really expected that it would lead the middle class to leave the city en masse. The idea was simply that it's good for Americans to own their homes. The government was going to help them own their homes, so the FHA was formed, and tax deductions were allowed on interest payments for mortgages. Home ownership was made easy, and everyone agreed that it was a great thing. Its effect, however, was to draw the middle classes right out of the city. Everyone was astonished when it happened, and suddenly a crisis was in the making. The crisis was created by that program. I'm not saying that middle-class people would not have left the city anyhow, but we wouldn't have had the tremendous outflux to the suburbs if home ownership hadn't been so cheap. The federal government didn't realize it was creating a crisis for the cities by encouraging home ownership.

It's a complicated world, far more complicated than any set of arrangements which can be devised or analyzed by a computer. It seemed like a good idea to control rents in New York City. But suddenly no building was going on. Then the government got into the building business. It turned out that the government wasn't very good at the building business, and ended up spending $45,000 for a four-room apartment in a low-income project. If we gave that poor family the $45,000, they could buy a home without a mortgage and still have money left over. But no! We are building low-income housing. Absolute madness. But it started and it's very hard to stop.

*What's your feeling on big business in government programs?
Do you think business has made some contribution?*

I don't think business has made any contribution to solve the urban crisis. I don't think it can. I don't think business knows when it's worsening the urban crisis or when it's solving the urban crisis. For example, you invent a telephone. One of the things about a telephone is that it permits members of a family to live further apart, because they can still talk to one another. If they didn't have telephones, members of a family would probably live closer together. Certain consequences would follow if family life in America were more tightly knit than it is today. The telephone makes it possible for family life to continue, but in a looser form. It has transformed the whole society in ways that were absolutely unforeseeable. Whether the total effect has been good or bad is practically impossible to say even now.

*Can you offer some guidelines on how to realize the benefits
of the unplanned process?*

It depends on what benefits you want. They're not really quantifiable; objective indices can be misleading. Back in 1958 and 1959, some Harvard professors carried out a very fine research project called the Hoover-Vernon research study on New York City. This study predicted what the city would be like in the eighties. As we approach that mark, it is clear that their economic predictions were unusually good. Their predictions of the occupational structure, the per capita income, the total population, and the population distribution of New York were almost uncanny. Their conclusion was that, as the city approached these figures, the citizens would be happier and more content, and everyone would be delighted to live here. They were right on all their objective indices and wrong on their conclusions. It is possible for objective conditions to improve, and at the same time for people to feel miserable about them. That's the nature of people. You send children to the best university in the United States and they burn it down, or try. Apparently they're unhappy. Hard to find out why they're unhappy. Very difficult, in fact.

One of my favorite sociological documents is a questionnaire at Berkeley. There was a poll of Berkeley students just a few weeks before Berkeley blew up. It asked students if they had any real grievances against Berkeley. Only a tiny percent had grievances. The questionnaire showed a happy, contented college population. Then the whole college exploded.

What do you think are the proper functions of government?

Let me point out one fact. If government were to do somewhat less, people would have somewhat more money of their own. All these programs are paid for by everyone—including poor people, who pay an awful lot in taxes of one kind or another. If some of the money could be saved in these programs, it could be put into people's pockets to make their own decisions on how to solve their urban problems. What do I think the functions of government are? Well, the classical functions: to preserve liberty, to preserve order, to improve the life of the citizens, however you define that.

Are we ill-served by the media?

We've always been ill-served by the media. I don't think this is a particularly new situation, although certain aspects of it are. I think the media are much better today than they used to be in relaying information. Forty years ago American newspapers contained very little information. Maybe that was good, since people didn't seem to be any less happy for knowing less about their problems.

The major national networks, plus the *Washington Post, The New York Times,* the major news magazines such as *Time, Newsweek,* and so on, represent a point of view of a new class, namely, the college-educated and relatively upper-middle-income class of this country. And that is a new phenomenon. I really don't know how important it is.

One reason why the media are a problem today is the rise of national network television. If *The New York Times* twenty-five years ago had been exactly the same as it is today, it wouldn't have mattered. It's a New York newspaper. New York is not the country. The same with the *Washington Post;* it's a Washington paper. What has happened with network television is that the three networks take their news from *The New York Times* and the *Washington Post,* thus making the views of local papers those of the entire nation.

The news magazines like *Time* and *Newsweek* are very much influenced by what the networks deem important, and vice versa. They don't want to be out of step. For example, it would not be feasible for NBC to say, "This is a big story," and *Time* not to publish a line about it. They'd both feel very peculiar, so they automatically respond to one another. The TV networks have acquired national influence.

A second problem is that as the American government gets more complicated and more bureaucratic, the media play a crucial role within Washington. They tell people what's happening in their own departments and in their own government. As the saying goes, you don't know what you've said at a press conference until the next day. Any department head who has given one knows that. The papers choose whatever interests them, and in turn the written word has an impact upon the two thousand subordinates in that department. They take the press report as a clue to what the department head wants. The media have become the internal communication network within Washington. For this reason, the people in Washington are probably overly sensitive to what the media say. I don't think the media have nearly as much influence as the White House and the Houses of Congress think. But the people in government certainly do believe that the media are powerful.

SELECTED WRITINGS OF IRVING KRISTOL

Capitalism Today (editor, with Daniel Bell), New American Library, New York, 1971. (Paperback.)

Confrontation: The Student Rebellion and the Universities (editor, with Daniel Bell), Basic Books, New York, 1969.

"The Foolish American Ism: Utopianism," *The New York Times Magazine,* November 14, 1971.

On the Democratic Idea in America, Harper & Row, New York, 1972. (Paperback.)

"Urban Civilization and Its Discontents," *Commentary,* November 1970 and January 1971.

"Urban Civilization Without Cities?" *Horizon,* Autumn 1972.

"Welfare: The Best of Intentions, the Worst of Results," *The Atlantic,* August 1971.

CHANGING INFLUENCES IN AMERICAN LIFE

DANIEL BELL

In his recent work Daniel Bell, professor of sociology at Harvard University, has concentrated on the use of sociological tools for social forecasting. Since 1965 he has been chairman of the Commission on the Year 2000, a social planning project sponsored by the American Academy of Arts and Sciences. He has also served as co-chairman of the Panel of Social Indicators in the Department of Health, Education and Welfare.

Over his long career Bell has worked as managing editor of The New Leader *and* Common Sense, *labor editor of* Fortune, *co-editor of* The Public Interest, *and a member of the editorial boards of* The American Scholar *and* Daedalus. *In addition to Harvard, he has taught at the University of Chicago and Columbia University, and has been a fellow at the Center for Advanced Studies in the Behavioral Sciences.*

FOR the past few years we've been hearing a lot of discussion about the future. Today I have news for you: the future is here. According to Goethe, what you wish for in youth, you'll get in middle age. Now we know that the things everybody wished for—cars, houses, television sets—can suddenly become a huge nightmare.

What I'd like to do today is to show you how social problems arise, and to identify some problems that in the coming years will be major themes of our social life. In analyzing social trends, it is wise to take account of four elements:

Basic structural trends—that is, changing social frameworks, or the changing social relationships people are put into.

The changing composition of social groups.

Changing social values and conceptions of legitimacy.

And that great bugaboo of all analysis: contingency, or accident, or chance.

Chance probably rules more of our lives than we care to admit; often it makes havoc of our efforts to cope rationally with the future. But I won't deal with it in this discussion because it cannot be formally analyzed. Contingencies can arise that are wholly unpredictable: today the obvious example is the ability of the Arab nations to exert pressure that nobody thought possible. Suddenly it turns out that we can't go 60 miles an hour because we don't have the gasoline for it. Even NATO is left on the point of collapse from lack of oil.

Since chance makes nonsense of predictions, what is the value of an exercise in social forecasting? The answer is that it shows us the constraints or limits of conscious human action (subject always to contingency) in changing our ways of life. By enabling us to see the results of a rational approach to our situation, it can give us a wider area of alternatives in determining the future within the hazards of chance.

STRUCTURAL TRENDS

In this country three structural changes—to a national society, to a communal society, and to a post-industrial society—have occurred in an overlapping sequence. The economic and social problems they have created, and the complications they present for our processes of government, are different in kind from those we have faced before.

A NATIONAL SOCIETY It was only about thirty years ago that the United States became a national society—meaning a society where events in one part of the country immediately trigger repercussions in every other part. We had always had a psychological identity as a nation, though it was tested only once, at the time of the Civil War. We were in fact the first new nation, a nation created by an act of conscious will through a revolution and a written constitution. But we did not develop national interdependence until the rise of modern transportation and communications.

We are a national society because we can go from coast to coast in five hours, because we have coast-to-coast telephone dialing, because our national weeklies are delivered simultaneously from coast to coast, and of course, because television provides us with a common framework of viewing.

If you consider economic interdependence alone, we actually became a national economy at the turn of the century. But it took the Great Depression to show us that we needed new techniques and new institutions—fiscal policy, or controlled monetary policy, or the regulation of security markets, or the regulation of labor markets—to cope with the new economic problems that were appearing. Franklin D. Roosevelt's New Deal was an effort to provide mechanisms for managing a national economy.

As we understand it now, the New Deal took certain kinds of powers which had been in the hands of the states and reinterpreted them through the commerce clause of the Constitution. In this way Roosevelt and his administrations created the lineaments of management for a national economy. Neither they nor their successors ever found ways to manage it smoothly, but in general the kinds of situations that led to the severe depression of 1929–1933 are not repeatable. The recessions we have gone through since have been different in kind and in origin. Today we couldn't talk about the economy without referring to gross national product and national income, yet these concepts were first proposed in Roosevelt's budget message of 1945. Our tools of analysis are very recent, and so is the Council of Economic Advisers.

In other areas, however, we have not even begun to develop institutions appropriate to a national society. Look at our administrative structure: this is probably the most dynamic economy in history, yet we administer it through what is almost a Tudor polity. Our political units—states, counties, townships, and so on—hark back to the days of Robin Hood. We have 3,000 counties; and though there are no Nottinghams and no Sherwood Forests around, there are sheriffs in plenty, with large amounts of patronage at their disposal.

The boundaries of our states evolved historically, and today they are inadequate as tax and administrative bases. One possible solution was outlined recently in the *Smithsonian* magazine, where a geographer proposed a new structure of 38 states on a natural regional design.* His plan calls for combining northern New Jersey, Long Island, and the New York metropolitan area into a new state called Hudson, while Buffalo would be part of a Midwest constellation.

Some kind of adjustment is essential in order to make the administrative structure of the country responsive to the problems

*G. Etzel Pearcy, "Brand-New Look for the States," *Smithsonian*, December 1973.

we have. Any society exists through its ability to provide effective services for people—down to garbage collection, mail delivery, and telephone facilities. When these things go out of whack, people are disoriented; they have a helpless feeling that things are falling apart.

Another weakness in our national society is that we still have no overall *standards* for health, education, and welfare—the major components of the quality of life. I'm not talking about national administration; no one proposes that kind of bureaucracy. But because we lack national welfare standards, for example, we have 50 different systems for deciding who receives welfare payments of how much. Consequently there is a huge migration of disadvantaged people around the country, a migration which tends to converge on New York City. The city today has one out of every eight families on welfare and a welfare budget of more than a billion dollars.

Over the years we've made efforts to create national welfare policies. Daniel Moynihan's guaranteed income plan, for example, was adopted by the Nixon administration but killed by Congress. One way or another the rest have failed too, and so have our attempts to establish a national health policy and a national educational policy. The lack of generally accepted standards in these fields breeds a pervasive sense of disorientation.

A COMMUNAL SOCIETY   The second structural fact about the United States today is that it has become a communal society—meaning one in which most social decisions must be public decisions, and in which most social benefits are regarded as group claims upon the community.

A fundamental dimension of our communal society is that more and more of the goods we need are public goods. Private goods are goods bought by individuals according to their own tastes and needs; public goods are standardized goods bought for us and distributed in a standardized way—prison uniforms, for instance. An obvious example of society's shift from private to public goods is defense weapons. In 1776 each soldier brought his own musket to fight the British; nobody manufactured muskets for the Army. Today nobody brings his musket to the Army (some people take a musket from the Army, but that's a different problem). The public purchase of weapons to be distributed through the government accounts for 2 or 3 percent of the GNP.*

Many kinds of goods that people demand today are essentially public goods. No one can buy a share of clean air in the marketplace; the quality of the air can be protected only by law. The increase of public decision making—of public authority—is not due to fading capitalism or creeping socialism; it is one of the fruits of interdependence.

A second dimension of the communal society is the rise of what economists call *externalities,* which are decisions generated by private parties that have external effects. Thus certain kinds of social costs generated by particular groups have to be borne by everyone. Pollution is a social cost generated by private parties but carried by the entire community. It accumulates from the emissions of automobiles, the waste products of industrial corporations, runoffs of municipal sewage, and even fertilizer on farms, which seeps into our rivers.

Again, the regulation of externalities must be a public function. An individual firm cannot undertake to rectify its own pollution without placing itself at a disadvantage in relation to its competitors. Some kind of public standards, public rules, are necessary in order to make pollution control meaningful.

A third aspect of our communal society is the fact that what people once regarded as expectations they now view as *entitlements.* More and more benefits have become claims on the community: the right to a job, the right to a minimum income, the right to health services, and so on. These are no longer thought of

---

*The total defense budget is about 6 to 7 percent of the GNP, but the greatest share is for salaries and maintenance of personnel.

as things to be acquired by the individual but as communal services organized in a communal way or guaranteed through some form of insurance.

A great source of friction in a communal society is the trend toward claiming entitlements on a group basis. Employment, for example, is often claimed in a context of quotas rather than of individual entitlements. In the New York City school system the conflict over entitlements is between the black community, which wants control of its schools, and the professional educators, who support a merit principle based on a standing or on examinations.

These are not questions of right versus wrong; if that were the case, most of our problems would have been solved long ago. They are issues of right versus right. What makes them more difficult is that the rights are demanded on a group basis, because individuals have organized to defend their entitlements.

A POST-INDUSTRIAL SOCIETY   The third structural change is that our society has moved from the industrial to the post-industrial stage; it is no longer a goods-producing but a service society. Today 65 out of every 100 persons are engaged primarily in services. By 1980 the figure will be 70 out of 100. This change has transformed the character of work in our country.

Most parts of the world are still pre-industrial. About 60 percent of their labor force is engaged in what might be called games against nature—extractive work, such as mining, fishing, logging, agriculture. These are occupations of low productivity, subject to the vicissitudes of resource depletion, wind, and weather.

A smaller part of the world is composed of industrial societies. In the Soviet Union, Japan, and the countries around the Atlantic littoral, most of the labor force is engaged in games against fabricated nature. These are economies of high productivity and growing national wealth.

In our post-industrial society, work takes the predominant form of games between persons—exchanges involving interpersonal elements. Essentially the technology is information; the key resource is human talent. And whereas an industrial society is largely male-work-oriented, a post-industrial society is equally male- and female-work-oriented.

A factor of crucial importance in a post-industrial society is the increasing centrality of theoretical knowledge. All societies have existed on a foundation of knowledge, but not of theoretical knowledge. Today our major industries—steel, auto, aviation, electricity, telephone—are still nineteenth-century enterprises, hold-overs from our industrial era. They were created by talented tink-erers who worked independently of the tradition of scientific re-search. Alexander Graham Bell was once called an elocutionist by that great theoretician of electricity and electromagnetism, Clark Maxwell. Bell was a speech teacher, and his invention of the tele-phone was in part an effort to amplify sound for students of elocu-tion and for deaf persons. His experiments with the telephone were independent of the work of people like Faraday or Maxwell.

The first modern industry was the chemical industry, since the manufacture of chemicals requires a theoretical knowledge of the macromolecules being manipulated. The science-based industries of the 1970s—electronics, optics, polymers—begin and end with theo-retical knowledge. Their products, such as the computer and the hologram laser, are derived from twentieth-century work in theo-retical physics and chemistry.

Consequently a major means of access to the technical and pro-fessional jobs of a post-industrial society is education. Knowledge becomes an extraordinary strategic resource. The husbanding of talent, and the maintenance of an adequate research and develop-ment base, are critically important.

CHANGING COMPOSITION OF GROUPS

The second element to analyze in identifying social trends is the changing composition of social groups. The source of one major development in this area was the revolution in agriculture during the period 1942–1970. It increased farm productivity by 7 or 8 percent a year and thereby reduced demand for farm workers. During that period, 25 million persons left the farms. Between 1960 and 1970, 1,000 of the 3,000 counties in the United States lost people from the farm to the city.

Some demographers and ecologists think that by the year 2000 the United States will have three large bands of population: Boswash, Chippits, and San-San. Boswash represents the 500-mile band between Boston and Washington, Chippits the zone from Chicago to Pittsburgh, and San-San the belt from San Francisco to San Jose or San Diego.

BLACK CONCENTRATIONS   One of the most startling consequences of the migration to the cities is the transformation of the black population, which for several generations had sharecropped Southern farms. Their movement from farm to city and South to North has resulted in concentrations of blacks in the centers of metropolitan areas like Detroit, Philadelphia, New York, Chicago, and St. Louis.

Usually when we think of the black situation we view it in modal terms, as if it were a single problem. But in reality the black population has bifurcated due to the extraordinarily rapid rise of a new black middle class. In 1960 less than 35 percent of black males had finished high school; by 1970 that number was over 55 percent. Such statistics indicate that for young blacks there is now a way into the society, and many, particularly those in the Northeast, have seized the opportunity.

On the other hand, a spreading number of blacks are almost permanently on welfare. In 1960 about 1.3 million blacks received welfare; today the total is more than 4 million. This tripling of the figure is partly a consequence of the black migration, in that many blacks who cannot find jobs in the cities are members of the old sharecropping population.

In the 1960s the movement of blacks into the ghettos resulted in riots when the young people, disoriented and embittered by their lack of progress, turned to violence. Today a substantial number of blacks have entered the political system: they are mayors of cities, members of Congress, town councilmen. But many more continue to live outside the society, and they will remain a potentially explosive group at least for the rest of this decade.

NATIVE-BORN WORKING CLASS   A second great change in the composition of social groups, and one that also has a potential for conflict, is the Americanization of the working class. Historically this country's workers have been largely foreign-born. Before World War I in particular, foreigners were imported in hordes to do our lower-paid dirty work. As late as 1950, 35 percent of the working class had at least one foreign-born parent. By 1960 this figure had dropped to 25 percent; by 1970 it was below 15 percent.

Now for the first time there is an American-born working class. Although their immigrant ancestors were willing to strive in poverty to create mobility for their children, today's working class wants mobility now. A large number of these young Americans did not graduate from high school, and they find themselves held back on the escalator to middle-class status. In their industrial plants they develop a sense of block mobility that contributes to industrial turbulence around the country.

PROFESSIONAL-TECHNICAL CLASS   The third major change in the composition of social groups is the rapid expansion of the professional-technical class. This group consists of people whose jobs require a high school, or more often now, a college diploma. If you plot the growth of the labor force from 1960 to 1980, the overall increase shows up as about 33 percent. The professional-technical component, however, has been growing at a rate of 66 percent. By 1980 there will be 15 million persons classified as professional-technical, making this the second-largest group in the labor force. (The largest will still be semiskilled workers, though their numbers are shrinking relative to the other groups.)

Yet the professional-technical group, the heart of the upper middle class, now finds that it is not so prosperous as it had thought. Increasingly its members are saying, "Our income has doubled, but we're not twice as well off as before. Why?" The reason stems from the very nature of a post-industrial society. One consequence of the shift from goods to services is that the price of services goes up at an increasing rate. They begin to cost as much as goods do, and it becomes difficult for all kinds of firms to maintain services.

Kahn's law (formulated by Herman Kahn of the Hudson Institute) states that when the per capita income of a country reaches about $4,000 a year, the standard of living of the upper middle class falls. This is largely because the kinds of services people were able to get before don't come so easily. For example, I can search through the whole of Cambridge, Massachusetts, where I live, without finding anyone to shine my shoes. And the costliness and scarcity of services have a more serious aspect than the simple disappearance of certain amenities. The basic fact is that inflation is built into the society. Over and above all other circumstances, whether they are a disastrous war or severe shortages, structural inflation steadily reduces the value of the dollar.

A goods-producing society does not have the same inflationary tendency. Here's why: Suppose the auto workers receive a 10 percent wage increase. How is that increase translated into unit cost? Because of the large number of jigs and fixtures needed for the assembly line worker to do the job, the automobile industry is a capital-intensive industry. The cost of labor is only 30 percent of the cost of a car. So the 10 percent wage increase translates itself into a 3 percent unit cost increase for the industry. And since the industry productivity is 3 percent or more, the 10 percent wage increase is not in fact inflationary; it produces only a 3 percent increase in unit cost.

Now look at a service industry: Suppose that New York City garbage men, or policemen or firemen, demand a 10 percent increase because the auto workers got it. For garbage, police, or firefighting services, the wage bill is 70 percent of the total cost. So a 10 percent wage increase translates itself into a 7 percent rise in the unit cost of the services. Since the productivity gain in these sectors has been about 1½ to 2 percent, the difference of 5 percent or more becomes the measure of structural inflation. Thus the shift from a production to a service economy, from an industrial to a post-industrial society, creates a structural inflation problem which can be overcome only by somehow finding methods to increase productivity in the service sector.

CHANGING SOCIAL VALUES

The third dimension for analysis in predicting social trends is the values of the society. Today ours are being modified in several ways.

ENTITLEMENTS One change in values which is increasing the areas of conflict within American communities has to do with entitlements. We are becoming more and more aware of our neighbors, in the sense that we cast a narrow eye on what our neighbors are getting. A source of this trend is the shift from economic to political decision making that occurred when the United States became a communal society. The question of where to locate a jetport, or whether to build a road through the ghetto or through the rich part of town, is no longer settled in the marketplace but in the political arena.

One great virtue of the market is that it disperses responsibility. If Du Pont introduces Corfam and spends 150 million dollars on promotion, Du Pont takes the loss if consumers do not like the product. The company simply misgauged the market. But in politics, everybody knows where the decision is made and whose ox is going to be gored. And everybody fights; people fight City Hall and they fight each other.

Today probably more Americans are participating in political life than ever before. They want to have a say in government. But involvement only seems to increase their helplessness, since by organizing politically they multiply the number of veto groups in the society. Board of Estimate hearings in New York City are thronged with spokesmen for hundreds of organizations, each one shouting, "Do what I say, not what the others say!" Compared with the old days of Tammany Hall, many more people in the city are now involved with the process of government. Yet the city is almost ungovernable because of the conflict of entitlements.

QUALITY OF LIFE   A second area in which American values are changing is our developing sensitivity to the things suggested by the phrase "quality of life." This new emphasis, which is partly attributable to the rise in American education and incomes, includes a growing concern for the environment and the ecology. Long before the Arab situation, the business forecasts of the oil companies were off because they did not anticipate the public's aggressiveness about the spoliation of the environment.

THREE PROBLEMS

These dominant trends in American life—structural changes to a national, a communal, and a post-industrial society, changes in the composition of social groups, and changes in social values—have produced three kinds of problems that will trouble our future. There is no mystery about their identity, because they are already upon us. They are the fiscal crisis of government, the management of shortages, and the overloading of the system.

COSTS OF GOVERNMENT   The expansion of government services and the shift of the society from economic to political decision making have created a situation where 12 million persons, or 16 percent of the labor force, are employed in government. Increasing amounts of government money are spent on externalities (for example, regulating activities concerned with the environment, energy, and land use) and social services (such as providing entitlements in health, public housing, and education). The costs of government are rising faster than the revenues produced by the economy.

What can we do about it? We can certainly try to reduce the huge amount of government waste, much of it a result of the antiquated administrative structures I mentioned earlier. The New York metropolitan area, for example, has approximately 1,400 local governments. They include park, sewage, water, and police districts, each with different taxing powers and different powers to control resources and take them away.

But even if we could eliminate all administrative waste, the increase in government services has created financial burdens which people are increasingly unwilling or unable to bear. In the main ours has been an individualistic society, where reward is based on effort and where the average citizen views taxes as money taken from him by Them. Though there is some truth in this attitude, taxes are necessary to purchase public services that people cannot buy individually. A rich man who is disenchanted with government's performance in maintaining law and order may go out and hire private guards, but most of us must depend on the police to provide security. Many citizens are becoming reluctant to pay the large taxes that these services require.

SHORTAGES   A second problem that will intensify in the future is the old question of the management of shortages. The very nature of entitlements raises the question of fairness, and the difficulty is that no system of managing shortages can be wholly fair to everybody.

Rationing can be accomplished by purse or by coupon. Rationing by purse would mean that the price of gasoline, for example, would go up to 80 or 90 cents a gallon. But then many people couldn't drive to work, even if they doubled up in car pools. Rationing by coupon, on the other hand, would require a great pyramid of appeals boards to adjudicate different classes of rationing priorities. And of course, many people would barter their coupons or sell them on the black market. Rationing by coupon is a bureaucratic nightmare.

No clear-cut answer is available to the question of what is fair and how you regulate it. Each attempt at a solution causes a large group of people to complain of injustice.

OVERLOAD The third of the major problems is derived from the other two: it is the overloading of the system. The concept of overload should be familiar to anyone working for a public utility. The political system is simply not equipped to handle the kind of multiple decision making now being assigned to it. Until recently, for example, there were 70 federal agencies concerned with energy in the form of coal, natural gas, oil, nuclear fusion, and so on. The sheer administrative load of coordinating such a system is unmanageable; things are done piecemeal, with no sense of the multiple repercussions in a national society.

The fact that these problems do not sound like science fiction, that they have the humdrum echo of our own everyday worries, demonstrates that the future is not an abstract point somewhere out in time. The future unfolds from structural tendencies in the present. By attempting to forecast our future problems, social scientists hope to sharpen our view of them so that if we don't like what we see, we will have a little more leeway to join forces and alter the shape of tomorrow.

QUESTIONS AND ANSWERS

Are all these problems caused by overpopulation of the world?

Overpopulation is a very real problem in some parts of the world. Clearly in India, southeast Asia, and parts of Latin America, rapid increases in population have eaten up all increases in productivity. In Africa, on the other hand, there is no problem; Africa is largely an underpopulated area.

Our country too has never really had an overpopulation problem. Our trouble is density of population: the unplanned bunching of people in metropolitan areas and the rise of infrastructure costs. It's been estimated that it costs $18,000 per person to provide services for an individual in terms of roads, water, sewage, education, et cetera. Each birth in the United States becomes a capital cost of $18,000. From 1945 to 1970 this country grew by 60 million persons. If you multiply 60 million by $18,000, you get a picture of the added capital burden.

It was only after World War II that the majority of people in this country could afford to buy their own homes. Veterans had to pay only 10 percent or less of a down payment, and in almost all cases interest payments on a house are deductible against taxes while rent is not. So a veteran could build equity in a house without much financial strain.

What happened was that small operators in the building trades field continued their traditional pattern of constructing single-unit detached houses in a gridiron arrangement. By doing so they multiplied the social costs: cost of parking space, cost of roads, cost of water, and so on. No one sat down and said, "Look, three different patterns are possible. You can have detached homes on the present suburban style; you can have cluster housing; or you can have high risers."

If these three possibilities are laid out on a matrix, you can compare the social costs of one with the other. But we've never done that kind of arithmetic for our cities, and the result is that we have an urban sprawl generated by an unthinking government policy.

So yes, population has played a role, but not in terms of numbers alone. It contributes to our problems in this country because of the kinds of densities that have developed.

What can you say about the reaction of other societies to the threat of shortages? And what about this society's reaction, particularly to the energy shortage?

Many societies—the Chinese and the Israeli, for example—are communally oriented. Their people believe that they have a common fate, and they will often make sacrifices on a voluntary basis.

England as a society performs well when faced with deprivation. The English have a high degree of civic responsibility, and because theirs is an island economy it lends itself to centralized control of rationing. The goods simply aren't on hand to rechannel through black markets. These two factors promote voluntary cooperation by the English in social crises.

As for Americans, we show a mixture of values where sacrifice is concerned. On the one hand, American society has always had a Puritan streak summarized in the work ethic, which in effect says that affluent living is morally wrong. To rephrase this dictum, it's not right that we, who are 6 percent of the world's population, should consume 30 percent of the world's energy. Some people welcome our current cutbacks because of this traditional Protestant moral fervor.

On the other hand, our society has become a hedonistic one where the major reward is pleasure. Today most people find their satisfaction in the income that their work produces—in the things they can buy. It is also an individualistic society in which each person thinks mostly in terms of "I want to do what I want."

So my answer is conditional. If a crisis requires short-term sacrifices, Americans will rally to it. But I believe that if the pinch continues, it will begin to get on people's nerves and the wear and tear will increase. Workers will turn to shutdowns and strikes because they feel disadvantaged, and throughout the society we will have increasing conflict.

A saving element in any crisis is the quality of a society's leadership. If you have leaders who are able to instill a sense of ethics, many private resentments can be overcome. It's very hard to see that quality of leadership emerging in this country.

Does the fact that we have more and more pressure groups, leading to escalated political decision making, create a situation of anarchy?

I think this is a crucial question; I would just reformulate it in one respect. I don't think the increase in political decisions is created by the pressure groups. Pressure groups are created by the increase of political decision making. The interdependencies of the society force people to organize politically to protect themselves against the consequences of political decisions.

Thirty years ago, this society was faced with a huge number of labor crises which almost pulled it apart. There were sit-down strikes, seizures of property—conflict on a scale far beyond anything that's happened in the schools in the last ten years. And yet we eventually worked out settlements through bargaining procedures. Bargaining has helped us arrive at some of the most important decisions the country has had to make.

Now we may have to devise methods for political bargaining—mechanisms for tradeoffs between community groups. In such a context each group would have to ask itself: "What do we want, and what are we going to give up for what we get?" New political bargaining machinery is one possible solution to the conflict and stalemates that stem from the multiplication of veto groups.

SELECTED WRITINGS OF DANIEL BELL

Capitalism Today (editor, with Irving Kristol), New American Library, New York, 1971. (Paperback.)

The Coming of Post-Industrial Society: A Venture in Social Forecasting, Basic Books, New York, 1973.

"Controversy: Is There a Post-Industrial Society?" *Society,* May 1974.

Toward the Year 2000 (editor), Beacon Press, Boston, 1969. (Paperback.)

NEW PATTERNS
IN THE
LABOR FORCE

❧

ELI GINZBERG

Eli Ginzberg, a specialist in manpower problems, teaches economics at the Columbia University Graduate School of Business. For twenty-five years he has directed its Conservation of Human Resources Project, a permanent research organization. He has published a huge body of work that examines labor resources from many perspectives, including those of technological change, education, ineffective performance, health, and opportunity for blacks, women, and young people. He has also served in government administrative and advisory capacities under the last seven Presidents. In 1974 President Ford appointed Ginzberg chairman of the National Commission for Manpower Policy.

TODAY let me describe some general but important new contours of the national labor force. The first is the marked increase during the 1970s in young males of prime working age. Essentially this is the baby boom of twenty-five to thirty-five years ago creating a bulge in the work force. There is a much larger supply of young workers, and it coincides with a pronounced cutback in the scale of the armed services.

The second point is that we have pushed the retention of young Americans in school not only to an optimal point, but in my private opinion, beyond that point. We now keep so many people in high school that 80 percent graduate with a diploma. Of that 80 percent, 50 percent or more go on to a junior college, post–high school training, or a four-year college. So 40 percent of young Americans are getting some postsecondary education. The only bright people who are not going on in any numbers are a certain group of women whose families are less inclined to invest in a girl's education than in a boy's.

Consequently in this decade there is not only a large supply of young workers available, but a large supply who have been exposed to schooling. I do not say that they are well educated; I'm making a distinction between being exposed to schooling and learning as a result of the exposure. But the length of time that people now spend in the educational process is impressive, and I suppose a little bit rubs off on everyone.

The third point I want to make—a point that is relevant for large cities all over the United States—alters our perspective on the first two points. The more that my associates at Columbia and I study manpower, the more impressed we become with de-aggregative studies. The generalizations that are based upon national figures provide only a clue to the composition of the labor force, because people live in particular locales, and even in subsections of cities. So it's really not much use to talk about the national unemployment rate.

For example, you have to roughly double the unemployment

rate to get the black unemployment rate; you have to triple it to get the youth unemployment rate. But for black teenagers in urban slums, you're up to a 35 percent range.

Now, if you pick married white males—which is the best part of the curve—and you compare them with the most vulnerable people in the labor market, the black teenagers, the rate is roughly the difference between 3 and 33 percent. That's a factor of 11.

So it's not useful to play with the national figures for very long before breaking them down. When you do, and when you look at the urban centers, you realize that the urban populations of the United States are by now heavily minority populations. New York City has one of the lowest proportions: blacks and Puerto Ricans are roughly in the 25 to 30 percent range. In Chicago, Detroit, St. Louis, and Pittsburgh the proportions are much higher. And a significant number of minority group members are still being very poorly trained in the public educational systems. Even in New York City with its high per capita expenditures for education, only about 15 percent of blacks come through high school with an academic diploma. And of course, those are the ones who go on to college, or junior college.

One result is that if New York Telephone is trying to get a group of high school people who have a reasonably good education into the system, and it relies on the New York public schools, it will be in trouble.

The next point is about young married women: 30 percent of them are now in the labor force, even though they have children under six years of age at home. Over the last couple of decades, a lot of women in their thirties and forties reentered the labor force. That was the first big increment. In the last ten years, it has turned out that young married women do not want to withdraw from the labor force for very long even after they have children. With the small family coming back into fashion—and we're very close to a two-child family—our large population gains are due to the fact that we have so many women in the child-bearing age group. Since they are having fewer children, they will be increasingly available for work.

I believe that in the next few years both the minorities and the women will keep aggressively pushing for a larger piece of the pie. The women will no longer be satisfied with conventional female jobs. In the U.S. Department of Labor, Office of Federal Contract Compliance, Order No. 4, which covers most large employers in the United States, compliance requirements based on sex have been added in every section where there were already requirements based on race. There's no doubt that the law will be heavily in favor of women.

Another prediction is that management and trade union leadership will have increasing difficulty in exercising discipline over the work force. One of the big problems is that neither the unions nor management can control the young workers, just as professors can't control their students and/or parents can't control their kids. The increasing challenge to authority runs up and down the system.

In good times, the situation is compounded by various industrial circumstances. For example, the automotive assembly line is a pretty lousy job; let's face it. Before the recession the auto companies had to have a supplemental work force for Mondays and Fridays, because if the regular people wanted to go fishing or hunting, they'd make it a long weekend. By working some overtime in someone else's shop they could make the same amount of money. They couldn't care less whether the supervisor wanted them back or not.

So the big automotive employers had to have a group of young college fellows who came in on Mondays or Fridays. They earned about $40 a day, and the exchange seemed mutually good. It gave the regular labor force some leeway and the college men a chance to earn some cash. Of course, the word was that you should never buy a car manufactured on Monday or Friday. But who cares about customers? They were lost in the shuffle a long time ago.

The next problem is that unemployment is likely to remain high for some time. Complicating the situation is the continuing inflow of women into the labor force, a movement which tends to increase the unemployment rate.

If the rate does stay high, I expect the unions to press strongly for shorter hours, longer vacations with pay, and more holidays. I have been surprised that labor has not driven harder over the last two decades to get the hours of work down.

As you know, experiments with four-day weeks have begun and may even increase because of the recession. In normal times I don't think the four-day week would work, for a special Ginzbergian reason. It is that the teachers would then want a four-day week, and parents would have to put up with their kids for three days a week, and that's impossible.

Congress has now moved on private pension plans and earlier vesting—a step that was long overdue, in my opinion. In many small and not-so-small companies a person could work for nineteen years and not qualify for anything until the twentieth, at which time the firm went out of business or had a long layoff and the employee got nothing. Since I believe that pensions are earned while you work, I am in favor of much earlier vestings. Then benefits will accrue to corporate personnel policy, because there will be earlier withdrawals from the corporation and more career shifts. I believe that every large company tends to accumulate too many people, and that any policy will increase efficiency if, without causing serious loss, it facilitates people's moving on. This kind of mobility is better for the individual, since it's tedious to be trapped for life in a single company. I'm in favor of using any device, including rules that allow employees to walk away with their money earlier, to give people a second crack at the world.

At Columbia we see more and more people who say, "Well, I don't want to keep working for XYZ Corporation forever. I'm an assistant vice president. It will take me another twenty years to get

to be a vice president. I think I'll get out and try something else."
So I'm a great believer in mobility, both for the corporation that's
losing the person, and for the individual who's getting out.

The trends that I have mentioned so far combine to create a
curious effect. From the point of view of the employer, the labor
market in the coming years will be a rich one, with many people
looking for jobs, and with most people having more education than
in the past. On the other hand, it will be a more restive and therefore explosive work force. Previously we have assumed that a
buyers' market produces a quiescent work force that makes little
trouble. Today and in the future, however, I believe you will see a
large number of people looking for jobs, and substantial discontent
at the same time.

Institutions can no longer assume that the old policies that were
so carefully worked out are necessarily the policies that make
sense now. The Army has begun to realize that practically all of
its procedures must be redesigned, because they simply do not fit
the kinds of young men we have today. And look at the Catholic
Church: a few years ago the synod split almost 50-50 on whether
celibacy was to be retained or not. Everything is up for grabs, and
even the two most conservative institutions in the world, the
church and the army, cannot operate as they used to.

In addition, I anticipate heated competition between or among
the men, the blacks, and the women for the relatively limited number of good jobs on the promotion ladder. Obviously there are not
an infinite number of good jobs around. Each organization has
relatively few, and the competition for them is going to be increasingly severe.

A problem in a different dimension altogether is the interface
in large cities beween security on the streets and getting and retaining an adequate work force. This problem is likely to become acute.
Some companies may decide to collect their people, move them to
the corporate locations, and then take them under escort—not
necessarily military escort—back to the transportation system. The

idea is not so extreme in some neighborhoods. I often come home from La Guardia through 97th Street, and New York Telephone has a little station there near Lexington Avenue. I wouldn't be caught dead there on the street at night, because that's what might turn out to be my permanent condition. In fact, I'm careful to see that the doors of the taxi cab are locked.

The next point is that we are entering a new era with regard to the amount of pressure the work force is going to exert concerning their work environment. I was in the Pentagon during World War II, and I can't think of a worse environment to work in than that barn. It didn't matter what rank you held or even whether you had a private office; it was a difficult environment. A certain amount of imagination about internal design and work space will be helpful at every level, from manufacturing to office work. It is clear that labor is pressing and will press increasingly hard along these fronts. The question is how quickly and with how much imagination management will move.

My impression is that there are several changes which are not too expensive that would contribute to an easing of some points of friction. I agree with Samuel Gompers that once you resolve a difficulty, there will arise a new area of discontent. Discontent is built into the situation. But there are more and less important areas of discontent.

I think you must anticipate greatly increased harassment from the federal government. The present not very liberal Supreme Court delivered a unanimous opinion several years ago that intelligence testing cannot be used anymore unless the company can prove that it is related to job promotion. Since the Duke Power Company couldn't prove it, the tests were declared discriminatory and thrown out. So, unless one has selection devices and promotion devices that are clearly validated as being work-relevant, they are illegal according to the Supreme Court. Since that was a unanimous decision, new appointees won't change anything.

We are beginning to enter a world in which the freedom for

both management and labor in wage bargaining will be substantially reduced. With large, powerful groups in management and labor, we can no longer operate this kind of economy without getting additional social control over wage bargaining and price structures.

The first point about productivity is the fantastic impact of modern technology upon most industries. (I have to be careful in talking to the communications industry, since it has moved backwards in my lifetime, in New York City.) The major impact has been in agriculture. We have been feeding the entire United States and many people overseas with 5 percent of our work force. It's a fantastic accomplishment; and we could probably get rid of half of our four million farm workers and never miss them, because they're only make-believe farmers, or they're semiretired. The effective work force in agriculture is probably 2 to 2½ million. That's the impact of technology.

It's important to note that two out of every three workers in the United States operate in what is loosely defined as the service sector of the economy. Only one worker in three is engaged in agriculture, mining, manufacturing, and construction, which together make up the goods production sector. We only use one-third of the work force in actually producing the goods. Two-thirds of all the people are involved in delivering the goods, losing them along the way, or stealing them and reselling them.

With only one-third of the work force in the goods production sector, it is obvious that there are few margins left for increasing the effectiveness of technology. But the sad part of the story is that in many parts of the service sector, the possibility of replacing labor with capital is severely limited. If you consider the medical service arena, roughly 65 to 70 percent of the total expenditures of hospitals are for wages and salaries. The health costs in the United States this year totaled more than 90 billion dollars, and an important reason they've increased so tremendously is that we have made very modest, if any, progress in manpower utilization over many years. We've almost doubled the number of personnel per patient in our general hospitals, from one and a half to three. If you've had the misfortune to be in a hospital recently, you will realize that doubling the personnel does not mean doubly good service.

This is one of the consequences of the difficulties in establishing standards of performance in the service sector. It is very hard to do, and therefore the potential for productivity gains in the service sector is more limited than most people realize. Progress in the service sector has taken an interesting form. We have returned the activity to the manufacturing area. For instance, when washer-women became scarce and it was hard to get domestic help, what we did was to move the industry into commercial laundries and self-service laundromats. When it became costly to go to the theater, we developed something called television which now serves as much of our entertainment. Thus we keep transforming what we want in the form of output by moving back from services into manufacturing. We do it in food preparation and elsewhere, and in the process we receive greater output with fewer people.

I believe the Chase Manhattan Bank has drawn some illustrations from the area of telephone service about the gains made over a period of time in increasing the amount of service per employee. Apparently you began to level off and were finding it increasingly difficult in recent years to continue to achieve those gains.

We are overwhelmingly a local, domestic service economy. How do we get and enforce standards of performance in the service end? How can we make sure that the tremendous number of people whom we pay to pick up the garbage actually pick it up? How do we know that those whom we pay to police the streets actually police the streets and are not engaged in some private rake-off system? How can we see to it that the people who are engaged to teach kids really teach them? We've increased the paraprofessionals in the New York school system by tens of thousands, and the evidence is that the kids learn less and less. So something is awry in the sense that we put more personnel in at one end, and we get less out at the other end. That's the nub of the productivity problem.

One of the most disturbing things is what we discovered several years ago in our Pentagon study. We had 1½ million people engaged in maintaining our fancy weapons system, and the equipment fell so much short of what manufacturers promised—it needed so much repair—that we were eating ourselves up trying to maintain it.

In conclusion, I would say that we have better-educated workers coming into the work force with much shorter fuses. They are willing to work, but they're interested in seeing the linkages between their work and their payoff. They are very here-and-now-oriented. The big fight in the unions is between the old men and the young men. The old men are interested in a large number of long-term security benefits that come with retirement or close to retirement. The young men want their returns now.

I think that the quality of the relationship between workers and supervisors will become increasingly a function of how well the boss performs. I think if supervisors earn the respect of the people who work for them, life will be easier. But nothing will be automatic anymore. As I indicated, I think there will be some rough times in the work place because different groups will be competing for the same jobs and for the limited number of better jobs. I think that's always been true, but the competition will get stiffer. And so I will end with the observation that the second half of the 1970s will be a difficult time. Business managers will have to earn their money.

SELECTED WRITINGS OF ELI GINZBERG

Business Leadership and the Negro Crisis, McGraw-Hill, New York, 1968.

Career Guidance: Who Needs It, Who Provides It, Who Can Improve It, McGraw-Hill, 1971.

Corporate Lib: Women's Challenge to Management (editor, with Alice M. Yohalen), Johns Hopkins Press, Baltimore, 1973.

Development of Human Resources, McGraw-Hill, 1966.

Educated American Women: Life Styles and Self-Portraits, Columbia University Press, New York, 1971.

The Future of the Metropolis: People, Jobs, Income, Olympus, Salt Lake City, 1974.

Manpower Agenda for Americans, McGraw-Hill, 1967.

The Manpower Connection: Education at Work, Harvard University Press, Cambridge, Mass., 1975.

Manpower Strategy for the Metropolis (with the Columbia University Conservation of Human Resources staff), Columbia University Press, 1968.

New York Is Very Much Alive: A Manpower View (with the Conservation of Human Resources staff), McGraw-Hill, 1973.

THE MEANING
OF MORALE
A Peace Corps Model

❧

W. WALTER MENNINGER

W. Walter Menninger was associate psychiatrist and senior psychiatric consultant for the Peace Corps from 1963 to 1971. He has also served as a consultant for VISTA and a member of the National Commission on the Causes and Prevention of Violence. He is now clinical director of the Kansas State Hospital in Topeka and a staff psychiatrist at the Menninger Foundation, a nonprofit center for psychiatric education, research, preventive care, and treatment. Menninger is a son of the late William C. Menninger, one of the organizers of the foundation.

I BEGAN looking into the subject of morale when I was one of two psychiatrists working full-time with the Peace Corps. Our task was to identify the kinds of stresses that Peace Corps volunteers experience overseas, and to figure out ways of helping them learn to tolerate those stresses.

Although morale is not a topic that you ordinarily find in the professional literature, it is a common term in everyday speech, particularly in business, industry, and other organizational and group settings. It is generally used to describe the prevailing temper or mood of a group, or of an individual's relationship to the group. It is not customarily applied to an individual's attitudes or feelings, yet in one sense I think morale can be considered as both an individual and a collective barometer of mental health. It is in this context that morale has a meaning in preventive medicine.

LESSONS FROM THE MILITARY

In thinking about improving morale in the Peace Corps, I looked at the studies that have been done for the military. My father was involved in this work as chief neuropsychiatric consultant to the Surgeon General of the Army in World War II. Anybody who's been in the service knows that there's always a lot of bitching and a lot of complaining. The constant problem is: How do you maintain morale? How do you keep people motivated to go on doing some very dirty work, or doing something they're not really interested in doing?

In World War II a number of lessons were learned about these questions. And my father discovered that almost all the lessons had already been learned in World War I and then forgotten. One of the tasks he set for himself was to make sure they weren't forgotten again.

Most people are not aware that 20 percent of the casualties in World War II were psychiatric. For every four people who were wounded or killed in battle, a fifth blew his top. The challenge was to identify and eliminate some of the casualties, both emotional and physical. When my father and his co-workers looked at the elements that go into morale—into the development of an effective spirit and temper in individuals and in groups—they were able to isolate certain key factors.

THE LEADER The first element that they distinguished was the quality of a group's leadership. You can take a bunch of mediocre soldiers and put a good leader in charge of them and have one of the best units in the Army. And you can take a crack unit of highly selected individuals and put them under a Captain Queeg, and they will be destroyed. This principle operates in any number of organizational or group settings. The manner in which a leader functions, and how effectively he handles his leadership role, can go a long way toward determining morale in the group.

THE MISSION Beyond leadership, there were two other elements that Army studies identified. One concerns the group's total mission. Each individual must have some understanding of why the mission is important and how his own work contributes to it. In World War II, for example, everybody was convinced that we needed to win the war, that we were threatened by the Axis Powers. And most people had a sense of how their jobs played a part in winning the war.

In an industrial setting, even a worker on an auto assembly line has to put his bolt in the right place. The car has something of the worker in it, because it would fall apart without that bolt.

One of the biggest problems that the country faced in the Vietnam war was the lack of public consensus on the value of the mission. In addition, most of the combat troops didn't really see what difference their participation made. A soldier on a search-and-destroy mission went out and searched and destroyed. He knew the Vietcong were there somewhere, because they faded away until he left and then came back in. The soldier's reaction was "What am I doing? What difference does it make?" It's easy to see why there were such tremendous morale problems in Vietnam, why men turned to drugs to try and escape from the boredom and futility.

A SENSE OF HOPE The third element of morale concerns the individual's personal experience—the evolution of his feelings as he becomes involved in an assignment. A person who takes on a task usually begins to change his sense of what he is as he comes to grips with the job.

When a soldier in the infantry went into combat during World War II, he was in combat until he got hurt, he got killed, or the war ended. He might have a temporary respite when a battle was over, but there was always another one coming up until the Axis Powers surrendered. An Army survey on casualties found a curious pattern: within a span of 90 or 120 days, there were two periods of increased injuries and deaths. One was at the beginning when new troops went into battle—which was no surprise, since inexperienced soldiers have higher casualty rates. But there was a second period of high incidence between 90 and 120 days. Analyzing the second period, the researchers found that it was a time when men became discouraged. "This is going on forever," they said. "There's no hope, there's no end in sight!" And casualties went up.

The lesson learned belatedly from this study was utilized occasionally in the Korean war and methodically in Vietnam. Soldiers in Vietnam were given a clearly defined, limited tour of duty under stress. Even during that period, they had intervals of rest and recreation outside the danger zone—leaves when they could get away to places like Thailand or Hong Kong. Giving a person a definite goal to achieve, after which he is guaranteed relief from constant threat, keeps alive his sense of hope.

PEACE CORPS MORALE

In the Peace Corps, where volunteers were working in foreign settings with little formal support, we wanted to know the same kinds of things that the Army had studied. What were the critical points in a tour of duty? What could we do to limit the "casualties"? What support could we give that would make a difference? Could we predict certain kinds of reactions?

We talked to Peace Corps volunteers who came back before their two-year service was up, and to groups who were finishing their tours of duty. Again and again we asked: "When were the times that were toughest for you? What happened then? How did you feel? What did you do about it?"

From this work we developed a graphline that we named the morale curve. Here's how it reflected a Peace Corps tour of duty.

Imagine that you are a group who have volunteered for the Peace Corps. You've passed security and gone through three months of intensive training. You have at least an adequate comprehension of the language in the place you're assigned to; you can make yourself understood. And you've been working at ways to apply some of your skills to help people in the developing countries.

CRISIS OF ARRIVAL   Let's assume that you're going to West Africa. Has anybody here been to West Africa? That's a good number; from your travel experience you can anticipate some of your feelings as a Peace Corps worker. We're going to send you to Ghana. And remember: This isn't something you've been conscripted for. You volunteered, because you felt that the Peace Corps offered a way for you to use your time to make a difference in the world. Now you've been given the stamp of approval, and we're assembling at JFK before getting on the 747 for Accra.

Let's start graphing your morale. We're going to identify certain critical points during the course of your experience. Right now at

Kennedy Airport, how do you feel? Just great? You're on top! So here you are at the beginning of the curve, right at the top.

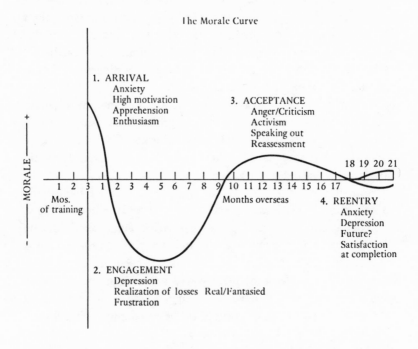

The Morale Curve

You're all high; you're feeling great. What's going through your mind? Does anybody have any reservations? Yes? What sort of reservations? You feel some anxiety? What are you anxious about? About what it's really going to be like? Well, that's easy to understand. For a couple of months you've been listening to experts tell you about Ghana, about the people, the climate, everything. You've had beautiful dreams about the place, but a few nightmares too. So some apprehension is mixed with your euphoria.

At Kennedy there were a few incidents of what is called "gang-plank fever," when volunteers who were not quite sure that they really wanted to go literally tripped on the steps up to the plane and sprained an ankle. One Peace Corps worker who fell up the steps ignored it and went on, and nobody else knew about it until three weeks later, when he was brought home delirious.

But gangplank fever is rare. Your group takes off from JFK without incident, and after an hour they start bringing cocktails. The booze flows; it's a party. At least you're together, and you can protect one another from being overwhelmed by worry. After dinner there may or may not be a movie, and you finally settle down. You sleep a little, but two hours later they flip everything up, turn on the lights, and it's breakfast time, though your stomach tells you that it's only 1 A.M. back in New York.

So you wake up with less than the greatest amount of sleep. You land several times before you get to Accra, but you arrive at last, and one of the first things you notice is that most of you are in the minority. It's an interesting sensation. Though you can get that feeling in New York by going up to Harlem, it's not really the same. But the Accrans are all smiling, and there are all kinds of new things to see. The health officer asks you to keep your seats as he walks through the plane from one end to the other with a spray to kill the mosquitoes that you ostensibly brought from Senegal.

Then they bus you to your place of residence, which is like a college dormitory, with a lot of concrete block formations (and mildew in the mattress: in Accra you never escape from the mildew). There's no hot water—and this is the big city. In the village where you're going, you will live the way the people live, and eat what they do.

So you go down to your first meal, and it's a marvelous piece of starchy cassava over which, to make it more palatable, they pour an oily, foul-smelling fish sauce that is one of the most effective weight-reducing meals I have ever tried. It's not because the calories aren't there, but because you don't eat. Or you eat just enough to keep going. As for the local atmosphere, the open sewers give it a characteristic fragrance.

Next you attend an indoctrination session, although you've already been through three months of indoctrination in the United States. You're set back down in the classroom to hear from the Ghanaians about how it is, and somehow their version doesn't seem to match what you've been told for three months. You wonder whether you've learned anything.

One of the speakers is a doctor, and he want you to know that the public health circumstances in his country are not like those in the United States. You can't drink the water out of the tap, and you must be careful about food. Ghanaians use human feces—night soil—to fertilize their vegetables, so you can't eat salads because you can't get rid of all the cysts.

That doctor is really concerned about your health. He draws you two blackboards full of the life cycles of the local parasites. He shows how the worms enter the body here and go up through the bloodstream and down through the lungs and all over the place. He wants to make sure this gets home, so he says, "Any time you're about to eat anything, just imagine that it's covered with a thin layer of shit!" This kind of indoctrination also helps weight reduction—and increases the number of volunteers who head back home.

When you started out from Kennedy only a few hours ago, you were at the top of the morale curve. There's only one way to go from the top, and you're headed there. All this is part of the crisis of arrival—point 1 on the graph. You're anxious, though highly motivated. You're still enthusiastic, but you feel progressively apprehensive. Rumors sweep through the dormitory: that some of you will have to live in tree houses, others in mud huts; that wherever you are, cobras nest in the kitchen and adders crawl into your sheets at night to get warm.

What can the Peace Corps do about the anxiety that builds and builds during the crisis of arrival? At first we had a high incidence of volunteers returning, until we discovered that the most effective solution was to get them out on the job. Sitting in the lecture hall at Accra, all of you are developing fantasies so lurid that the reality will be pale. To reduce anxiety over something unknown, there's no substitute for making it known.

CRISIS OF ENGAGEMENT So we began to speed people out to their assignments, and it helped; their anxiety did diminish as they were faced with real problems instead of imaginary ones. Then what do you suppose happened to morale? Did it go up? No, it didn't.

Here's a statement by one of the volunteers who happened to go to Latin America:

> *I entered my town on Friday, all alone, with a ranking of number 19 out of 27 in my Spanish group. The first few days were hell. I never felt so frustrated, disconsolate, depressed, and lonely in all my life. My initiative waned; my enthusiasm flopped. I became tired of Spanish, and the heat spattered me at an annoying rate. Traffic horns beeping all night outside my window kept me awake, and the food in this town left much to be desired. If I hadn't told myself that I wasn't a quitter, I might have quit then.*

It's depressing to discover that the world isn't ready to let you save it. You struggle to get oriented—to learn a new set of cues, in an unfamiliar setting, sometimes in an unfamiliar language, usually in an unfamiliar cultural situation. For example, no sensible Latin American woman goes around unchaperoned. So what is the gaucho to assume about the character of these young Peace Corps women?

Or take the volunteer who's supposed to help with community development. The village leaders listen politely to his suggestions and nod, recognizing that gringo Americanos bring money and bulldozers and other good things. When the volunteer explains in his halting Spanish that he is a different type of American, they don't believe it. But they never show up to work on the projects he tries to get going. He becomes less and less energetic, more and more frustrated, more depressed.

This is the feeling tone of what we termed the crisis of engagement—point 2 on the morale curve. It usually set in about 90 to 120 days after the volunteers had been on the job. It was a time when they had to face their losses and the limitations of their circumstances.

In the crisis of engagement a volunteer became fully aware of what he had lost by taking on the assignment. He was giving up not only the comforts of ice cream, steak that can be eaten rare, good detergents for washing clothes, and water that doesn't have to be boiled, but time—time when he might have been accomplishing more in his own country. Even worse, he had to face the loss of his romantic fantasies about his assignment. The depth of this crisis depended in part upon the degree to which the reality fell short of the dream. Anyone who has to give up some hopes and illusions suffers a loss, and any loss hurts, psychologically or physically.

One volunteer in Africa said:

> When we were in training, it was generally thought that the difficult part would be living in squalor and tolerating extremes. Ironically, in fact it is the mediocrity of everything which is the most depressing. Living in poor surroundings but not heroically so; facing a daily routine more boring than one could possibly imagine; being welcomed into the society and yet not being accepted into it; adapting to a monotonous climate which never changes, but is always hot; learning the delicate balance between push and patience.

As the volunteer gives up his fantasies, so also must the community, which prompts a bit of mutual depression. It is at this time that the local people are forced to recognize that the volunteer really is a different kind of American. He isn't the sort who brings those good things into the village, or spends all kinds of money. Indeed, he often drives a hard bargain in the marketplace.

During this trying period when the volunteer was coming to terms with his losses, he was also discovering the constraints on his power to change things. He didn't know the right place to make inputs to get the simplest problem solved. He lost all kinds of energy trying to go from here to there.

One volunteer in Colombia said: "I've got to do something! These mosquitoes are driving me crazy, I'm going to do something about the mosquitoes." So he got some oil (not without difficulty), went out of town three miles, and sprayed it on a pond. He told his partner what he had accomplished, and the partner said, "Come with me." They went out of town a mile in the other direction, came over the crest of a hill, and as far as they could see was swampland.

The volunteers developed a pervasive feeling of "So what?" And who could they blame? Whose fault was it that they were where they were? In their discouragement and depression they sometimes stopped taking care of themselves and got sick.

As you would expect, during the crisis of engagement there was again a peak in the number of volunteers returning. What can be done for people who are in this morale slump?

One volunteer told us, "I went AWOL, and it helped." He had assumed that the others in his Peace Corps group were doing great things in the next village, saving the world and killing mosquitoes, while he flopped at everything he tried. But when he went to the next town and met his friend, he discovered that his friend was in the same bad shape. They commiserated over beer (alcohol consumption goes up during this period), and they found that each of them had learned a few tricks the other didn't know. As they compared notes they developed a little perspective and realized that their experience had not been a total loss, and by the time they parted they had regained a sense of commitment.

To help people cope with the crisis of engagement, we found that the best thing we could do was to bring the group back together for a short while. This gave them an opportunity to exchange stories and get some distance from their immediate tasks. It pulled most of them out of the doldrums—and when they emerged, they entered what we came to regard as a kind of golden period.

Back in their villages they had painfully learned a few of the ropes, and they were able to invest more of themselves in the assignment. They overcame a few obstacles; they got some project going which began to show gains. It dawned on them that their tour of duty, though short on romance and adventure, would not be a complete waste of time.

CRISIS OF ACCEPTANCE   Then somewhere around the midway point, the volunteers entered a new phase. Lacking the diversions that they had had at home—television, movies, a great variety of social outlets—many Peace Corps workers experienced a society in solitude for the first time. They looked at it and themselves in a new light, and many of them began to ask, What am I doing here? What does it all mean? What right do I have to try to change these people? When I leave, who will carry on what I am doing? Am I justified in stirring up aspirations which may never be fulfilled?

They began to notice good things about the people whose country they were living in. The family life seemed to have more integrity than much of the family life back home. And that mañana philosophy seemed to work better than Americans would expect; things did get done tomorrow, or sooner or later—so why rush?

By this time the volunteers had enough clout in the community to speak up and get a hearing. When they looked at things that weren't right, they could decide to do something about it. They had been there long enough to know where the power was, where to touch base in order to get results. Their anger grew; often they took direct action.

This was the crisis of acceptance. It was the period when Sargent Shriver received the stormiest letters from the volunteers. It was the period when a volunteer would hike down to see the minister of the interior, tell him how corrupt the school principal was, and suggest that the minister shape the country up.

Morale was fairly high during the crisis of acceptance, though the predominant feelings were anger and activist energy. But out of the crisis came a maturation of the volunteer's expectations. He began to sense the real values in what he was experiencing, as opposed to the naïve values he had started with. At last he resolved his sense of identity in his alien surroundings. He began to formulate the things he might reasonably expect to accomplish, the things he might reasonably demand of himself. One volunteer said:

> *I am as idealistic as I ever was, but not fanatic. Nobody, not even the Peace Corps, is going to solve the world's problems in my lifetime. So I've learned to do what I can; above all, keep myself open to the needs of other people, but without getting into a stew about it.*

CRISIS OF REENTRY After the crisis of acceptance came another period of highly effective functioning. Then in the case of a self-limiting experience like the Peace Corps, there was a fourth crisis as the volunteer's tour of duty came to an end. We called it the crisis of reentry because it represented not just a termination, but an anticipation of another major change in life.

Now the volunteer's feelings were a volatile mixture of anxiety about the future, satisfaction at having fulfilled a commitment, and depression at giving up a job that had become part of him. At this point—number 4 on the graph—the morale curve forks, to indicate that an individual's morale could be slightly on the plus or slightly on the minus side depending on his particular situation and his plans for the future. At that point, as the volunteers headed for home, they started over again on the morale curve.

MORALE CURVE APPLICATIONS

When those of us who had worked on it took a closer look at the morale curve, we began to realize that it could be applied to other situations besides a Peace Corps tour of duty. We would start by discussing an individual problem and discover that we were actually talking about the curve again. We saw it operating in miniature in the training of some VISTA volunteers in a mental hospital. The curve is extensible or contractible; it can be useful in interpreting student—and faculty—ups and downs through the college year, and it can chart the four-year college cycle, which might be described as freshman anxiety, sophomore slump, junior activism, and senior disorientation.

Whenever a person takes a new job or changes his life situation, his sense of himself undergoes changes that produce the stresses reflected by the morale curve. How intensively an individual responds to the pressures of adjustment depends on his expectations, his capacities, and the outlets available to him for achieving satisfaction and expressing feelings. Of course, when the new job or identity has no definite end point, there is no obvious crisis of reentry. A very rough expectation, however, is that the final evolution and solidification of the new sense of self will take about two years.

Thus it is my experience that the morale curve has a contribution to make in individual counseling and in administrative policy making. Self-knowledge is an important resource for organizations as well as for individuals, and both can benefit from tools that provide a perspective on people's involvement with their work.

PRODUCTIVITY AND THE KNOWLEDGE WORKER

~

PETER F. DRUCKER

Peter F. Drucker, who was born in Vienna, was educated in England, took his law degree in Germany, and began his career as a banker in England. He came to the United States in 1937 as American editor for a group of British newspapers and as investment adviser for a group of British banks. He soon established himself as a consultant, writer, and teacher. He has been an adviser to businesses such as General Motors, Sears, Roebuck, and General Electric, and to government agencies in the United States, Canada, and Japan. His writings have brought him recognition as a dynamic theorist in the conservative tradition. From 1950 to 1972 Drucker was professor of management at New York University. He is now professor of social sciences at Claremont Graduate School in California.

M OST of you are young people who will be around and active for quite a while. What are some of the areas that need your work, that challenge you as managers in this company and this society? I believe that the greatest immediate need of business management today is to go to work again on productivity. It is an area which we took for granted fifteen years ago, but it will be the central economic problem for all the developed countries in the next fifteen to twenty years.

We can no longer assume that we understand productivity and know how to improve it, because there has been a tremendous shift in the work force. Fifteen years ago the central productive factor was the manual worker. Today the cost center (which is not quite the same thing as the central productive factor) is the knowledge worker. Knowledge workers do not work with their hands, but with what they supposedly have between their ears. They utilize concepts and theory rather than brawn or manual skills. The alphabet is not a manual skill; it's a concept, a highly abstract one. (I wish more file clerks had learned it.)

Knowledge work is not elevated work, necessarily. There is a lot of unskilled knowledge work around, but it is not manual work. There is also a great deal of work in which we have to marry manual skill to high abstraction. Computer programmers, for instance, are knowledge workers, not terribly advanced. Any junior high school girl can learn to be a programmer—not a systems engineer, but a programmer. It is a knowledge skill requiring a high degree of abstraction, but at the same time it is semimanual, and as a manual task it is almost unskilled. Very few manual occupations have that short a learning period and that steep a learning curve. Within six to eight months a trainee can be a good programmer, and six months later a very good one. The same is true of medical technologists, who are possibly our greatest labor shortage today. And so on.

MEASUREMENT PROBLEMS

Although our center of gravity has been shifting to knowledge work, we don't know how to make knowledge work productive. When I say we don't know, I mean it literally, because we have no idea how to measure knowledge output. We can easily measure how many pairs of shoes go down an assembly line, but we can't measure, say, the output of an engineering department. Yet there are few things less pleasing than an engineering department which with great elegance and diligence and speed turns out drawings for the wrong product. How do you measure that? By the time you find out, it's too late.

We have made manual work measurable, though it took some doing. If you had talked productivity of manual work a hundred years ago, no one would have understood you. The word "productivity" as applied to output did not emerge until around 1900. It was only after we had learned, through scientific management, that productivity is not a matter of working harder but of working smarter that we could begin to theorize about it. Our great grandparents took it for granted that the only way you get more output is by sweating more, and that isn't productivity; that's incompetence.

It was the great generation between the Civil War and 1900 which developed the idea that productivity is the design of the job and not the sweat of the workingman's brow. We haven't reached that stage in knowledge work yet. We know only that the productivity of knowledge work is quite different from that of manual work. We do not see any reliable sign that we know how to manage knowledge work and how to make it productive.

In fact, from where I sit on the outside there isn't the slightest sign, in the terms which an economist would accept, that anything has happened in the labor force. There isn't a sign that productivity has been improving. There isn't a sign that profitability has been improving. There isn't a sign that any great change has occurred.

And yet we have been undergoing one of the greatest changes in the labor force on record. Only the transformation of yesterday's laborer into today's machine operator, which is a change of 1900, can be compared in magnitude. That change was accompanied by a tremendous outburst of productivity, but the current shift in the labor force has preceded our knowledge and our ability to manage.

Yet without an understanding of knowledge work we cannot have effective economic policy. Every one of the developed countries today suffers from inflation that it cannot control and has no way of managing. But nobody knows anything about the relationship between productivity and the macroeconomy of economic policies. And that is at the root of our problem. For reasons nobody understands, productivity stopped growing in this country around 1964. We don't know how to get it going again, except maybe through heavy doses of unemployment, which is highly toxic. Moreover, unemployment doesn't really work. There are countries in which heavy doses of it have not had an impact on productivity, and in our country it has had none since the early sixties. So we don't know.

We must increase the profitability of our economy for two reasons. First, the new demands associated with the environmental movement will multiply the costs of production. If you have hopes of expanding our educational or health care programs, forget them. The environmental demands will eat up any increases in gross national product, let alone any increase in tax capacity that we can foresee in the next ten years. Indeed, we must consider the extent to which environmental needs are a threat to the poor people of the world. If the costs of an economy go up faster than productivity, the poor suffer. It invariably happens, no matter what the economic system.

The environmental need is great, but the danger is also great, and the people who make environmental claims without thinking the priorities through are a menace. The time has come to ask: Where do we go to work? In what areas can we achieve results?

And how much are we willing to spend? What is the payoff level? It's too risky otherwise. It's also risky not to do something about the environment, but we cannot proceed by sloganeering. The cost structure of meeting environmental needs will go up very rapidly. There is no way to pay for them except by high prices or higher productivity. The idea that business profits can pay the bill is a joke, because they amount to 5 percent of the GNP. Minimum environmental costs are probably 30 or 40 percent.

Also let me say that the profits reported in the last five years are an illusion; American business has been running at a loss because of inflation. If you adjust depreciation charges to inflation—in other words, if you maintain the physical plant—you have no profits. If we kept our books in constant dollars they would show none.

Business needs more profit not only to apply toward environmental costs, but because the number of people entering the labor force now is significantly larger than it was a few years ago. The babies born in the big baby years from 1947 to 1957 are entering the labor force. We need to create jobs each year for three to four hundred thousand more young people than in the sixties. A job in the American economy requires a $15,000 to $25,000 capital investment. This has to come out of capital formation, which is another word for profit.

The only feasible solution to our economic problems is to raise productivity, and the only way to accomplish this is by raising the productivity of knowledge work. How can we do it? I can give you guesses, but that's all. No one has any answers, if only because we can't define the productivity of knowledge work. We can define and measure the productivity of billing clerks and telephone installation men, but not of managers, engineers, computer programmers, or medical technologists—the skilled and semiskilled knowledge workers who are where the growth is and is going to be. We cannot measure productivity in the elementary school classroom, though there seems to have been very little increase in it over the years.

As for hospitals, there has probably been a net decrease in productivity. Judging crudely by how many patients walk out, it takes more people per patient today to dispense what is not better medicine or better patient care.

We will have to solve these riddles of productivity helter-skelter, by muddling through them. Later we can develop a good, intellectually satisfying theory, but the doer traditionally comes before the philosopher. Philosophers codify what has already been achieved—an important role but not a pioneering one. We will learn about the management of knowledge work by making mistakes and running down blind alleys, and it will be people like you who do it.

INNOVATION AND INSTITUTIONS

A second challenge in the area of productivity concerns the higher levels of knowledge work. Management will have to learn how to use its trained professional people to make the large institution innovative—to develop and market new ideas and new inventions.

During the last seventy years, managers spent a lot of time and thought on learning a little bit about how to manage—that is, how to achieve results which they defined. Management has given its name to the whole discipline of making institutions perform. Many people believe that internal order is the essence and the end-all of management. Yet managing an institution is only one aspect of its performance.

There were good reasons, however, for this emphasis on internal order. Sixty years ago in the heroic age of Theodore Vail, nobody had ever tried to do what your great grandparents in the Bell System attempted—namely, to manage a large, complex human organization. It was a new thing under the sun. Armies, the oldest large organizations, were always short-lived; the soldiers disbanded after a campaign for the simple reason that the army could not feed them. From the Persian host that invaded Greece almost

2,500 years ago to the troops of the Civil War, armies were temporary and their structure was uncomplicated. There was no need for large permanent organizations, and certainly not for organizations that brought together people with different skills for joint performance.

In the late sixteenth century one of the greatest painters of the Western tradition, Peter Paul Rubens, was accused of witchcraft by the Inquisition. Only the fact that he was the court painter of the Spanish regents of the Netherlands, and had exceedingly good connections both at court and in the church, got him off without serious trouble. The charge was that he had some sixteen painters in his workshop. Everybody knew that it would require supernatural help to manage so many highly skilled people working together. The natural organization was to have one man do the work with the help of assistants—a system which is still found in the European university today. The professor has assistants, but he is the only worker, so to speak; the others just hand him the tools. Ninety percent of the troubles of the European universities are caused by this organization. Yet a hundred-odd years ago it was the only one that people could manage, and simple though it was, it didn't work with more than four or five assistants. Sixteen first-rate painters in a joint team organization was witchcraft.

It was not until the railroads came that we had permanent establishments in which many men with different skills and knowledge had to work together. In those days, even government agencies were small. There is a charming description of the British Home Office in one of Anthony Trollope's novels about Victorian England. It was the period during which the Home Office revolutionized English local government, creating one of the greatest constitutional changes in that country's history. And here was the all-powerful Home Office, the British Ministry of the Interior, with one minister, an anonymous assistant secretary, and a few people who copied documents with quill pens. That was it: the Home Office of 1870.

Lincoln's war office consisted of twenty-one employees, including telegraphers. Hospitals were merely chaotic places where the poor went to die. In 1914 when World War I broke out, there was no university in the world that had as many as 5,000 students.

The large, complex organization is a creature of this century. I'm not saying that we've learned how to run it well, but at least it doesn't fall to pieces every five seconds. Lincoln's war department did, because they couldn't manage twenty-one people. Nobody could figure out who was supposed to do what; in 1860 it didn't occur to anybody that a job could be defined.

Now we face an era of exploding technology—one like the great period of 1856 to 1914, in which a major new invention, resulting in major new industries, appeared on an average of every seventeen months. Fifteen years ago the telephone looked like a secure monopoly, but no longer. Don't believe it, incidentally, when people talk about the speed with which technology travels these days. It moves slowly compared with the way it used to spread. For example, the one significant advance of the Middle Ages in health care was the development of spectacles. Friar Roger Bacon in the wilds of Yorkshire, which in those days was boar and bear country, made his experiments in 1282, and by 1285 glasses were common both at the papal court in the south of France and at the court of the sultan in Cairo. Three months after Edison had finished work on his invention in Menlo Park, New Jersey, they installed Edison light systems in London. Three months after Alexander Graham Bell filed his patent, an English telephone company sold telephones in London. Few technologies travel that fast today; what does move faster is information.

Today's innovations may not originate within the large enterprise, but they have to be developed and marketed there. That's where money and people, the two necessary ingredients for development and marketing, are located. It is in development where the money is needed; not in the invention or the innovation itself. And it is people that are needed for development and marketing—trained, skilled professionals. Today they are found in large organizations if only because the tax system works that way in all developed countries.

The large business will have to learn to be innovative, which it has rarely been. You created one of the few exceptions fifty, sixty years ago when you set out to make innovation possible in a large enterprise that had to follow uniformity over a continent. You succeeded by forming Bell Labs, but no other companies have yet adopted your basic thinking. On the whole, large institutions are not innovative; they can modify but they cannot innovate. Almost everything that's new looks so small. If we didn't know that new-born babies had a fair chance of being adults eighteen years later, we wouldn't pay much attention to them.

If you run a fifty-, eighty-, or hundred-million-dollar division, you have enough work to do. There's always a crisis, and it always has to be taken care of yesterday. And so you don't put your good men to work on innovations—on the things that are only important rather than urgent.

Somehow we have to learn to make the large organization innovative. The Bell System taught us the basic lesson that innovation requires a separate innovative organization which must be integrated into operations. This is not an easy thing to do. Bell Labs was not an instantaneous success, but a number of chief executives believed in it and worked at it. It didn't really get going till the early 1930s as a productive organization, after almost twenty years of very hard work. It turned out a lot of brilliant technical things before that, but it had little impact on the company and on communication services.

Creativity is not our problem. We can get more ideas out of a meeting in an hour than we can work on the rest of our lives. Our problem is to do something with ideas. I want to see a little work, and a little achievement.

THE MANAGER AND THE KNOWLEDGE WORKER

Let's look now at the knowledge worker whom you will have to manage. The first person you must manage is yourself, because you're also a knowledge worker. The most neglected area of management is the effectiveness of the manager. The books talk a lot about how he manages others, but very little about how he makes himself effective.

By the nature of his occupation, the knowledge worker must be both a producer and an achiever. He is not satisfied with making a living, and he'd better not be or he soon ceases to be productive. Knowledge is a peculiar resource. If it does not improve and grow, it deteriorates rapidly. It cannot be stored. What can be stored is information. The knowledge worker is therefore right in aiming for a career instead of a living.

A few years ago when there was a proposal to locate a department store with 800 jobs in Harlem, some people in that neighborhood opposed the project because a department store doesn't provide any careers. These were people who desperately needed incomes and jobs. The mayor assured them that a department store job is an honorable one, but that wasn't their point. They asked: "Well, where does it get us?" And they were right. A department store job gets you nowhere, except into the department store basement.

This is a change in the basic attitude of people who are uneducated, who are poor, and yet who want more than just a living. You may say that their objections were unrealistic, and that's true, but they were still right, fundamentally. We are far gone on the road toward intellectual arrogance. We must realize that we have to make it possible for the black girl who becomes a health aide to become a medical technologist. And if she wants to work even harder, to become a nurse—or a doctor, if she wants to. We will have to learn not to say: "But you didn't take business English in fourth grade." It's something I remind my colleagues about, but I don't make much impact. They still turn people down because of pieces of paper. We must overcome this tendency if we want our society to survive.

The people in Harlem only reflected the attitudes of the more privileged; they just did not want to be discriminated against. The privileged people, the knowledge people, have had the benefit of a tremendous investment in education. And they don't want a living; they want to make a career and a contribution. Fifty per cent of the male population now goes to school beyond high school. They are not a privileged elite; they are the successors to the honest and decent skilled worker. But they must have the career and achievement opportunities, and it's our job to open up these opportunities. The knowledge worker, in other words, is a different kind of worker, not only in what he brings to work, but in his expectations. We will have the challenge of making the knowledge worker productive and achieving.

You at Bell have done a pioneering job in what you call "job enrichment" for manual and clerical employees. Are you doing anything comparable for managerial, professional, and technical people? I doubt it. And yet that's where the need is greatest. That's where jobs for young people are most tightly confined and defined, are smallest, are least challenging, and above all do not permit learning.

We don't allow young people to learn the two most important things they must learn. First, they have to get the sense of achievement; they have to do something they know they aren't really capable of doing. Anybody who has ever done so never loses the thrill. It is the only motivation for knowledge people. Secondly, they have to learn what they cannot do. All of us have to fail—to crawl back with our tail between our legs and say: "Damn it, I can't do it. This is beyond my capacity." If you don't have those twin experiences, you haven't learned anything. In fact, you cannot really learn. We are depriving our young knowledge people of these learning experiences. We are treating them the way we treated yesterday's assembly line worker, and this will lead to a demoralized knowledge force.

We will also have to accept the fact that in most knowledge work a person needs a second career after twenty years. The great demographic achievement of this century is not the extension of life spans but the extension of the working life span. Two generations ago most people went to work at age twelve or fourteen, but they did not have a working life expectancy of more than twenty to thirty years, particularly on the farm. The farm before the automobile, the tractor, and electricity was a crippler. It still has an accident rate about ten times that of the worst coal mine (it used to have one about a hundred times as bad). It was also terribly hard work. By their late thirties people were disabled by accident or arthritis, and they were tired and worn out. As for the ditch diggers who were hired a little earlier to build the transcontinental railroads, they had an average working life of eighteen months. After that they were gone, finished off by syphilis or hard work or accidents or drink. Nobody expected them to last any longer.

It may surprise you to look at the older pension plans, such as the early civil service plans. Not a single one of them was designed to give a pension to the retiring employee. They were all plans to look after the widow and the children. The oldest we have—an Austrian plan of 1803—had no pension for the employee himself. If he lived to age sixty-five, the emperor would consider a pension, but the case rarely arose. There was a vested annuity for widows and children right from the start, and it remained unchanged till 1938, when Hitler came into Austria. By then it had become a little archaic, but it could still be made to work.

People didn't die, necessarily, but they became unable to do full work. Today we expect most people at age sixty-five to be physically and mentally in working order: not in perfect shape, but capable of doing most kinds of work. That's a tremendous change. We have responded to it by keeping people in school much longer, not because they're learning anything in school but because we don't really want them in the labor force. Their working life would be too long. And even the forty-five years we now have for the knowledge worker is probably too long. There's something very funny about knowledge work. Manual workers in early retirement move to Florida and are happy not to do anything. Manual work still tires. Knowledge work exhilarates and excites, and a fellow gets into the habit of working; he can't kick the habit. At age forty-five, however, he has lost his zest. This isn't true of the few who get to the top and of the few who really excel. But it is true of 90 percent of the work force. In business this problem is least pronounced, because business has the greatest job mobility of all our major institutions. People can move from one company to another, and frequently do. There is far more mobility in middle management in business than, for instance, in government or in the university. Half of the college teachers who started out as very bright fellows are bored and tired of it by age forty-five. They go through the routine and become poor amateur painters, which is better than taking the way of the bottle or the psychoanalyst's couch.

In knowledge work the good market researcher at age twenty-nine is really very excited about the toy market. But he knows all about the toy market by the time he's forty-five, and it doesn't excite him any more. A market researcher is all he wants to be and all he can be in this business, not only because the opportunities at the top diminish arithmetically, but also because few people really want the demands of a top job. They want to have the opportunity to go to the top, but they don't want the job. And the market researcher at age forty-five retires on the job, and so do many of my faculty colleagues.

We will have to work hard and systematically at finding second careers for knowledge workers. Employers are always saying: "Jim was such a good man, and now he's burned out." Jim isn't burned out; he's just bored. Move him to another place and he'll come to life.

In my twenty years at New York University I placed about two hundred ex-military officers. The military has a rule that you reach a certain age and if you don't get beyond a certain rank, out. So I placed a lot of lieutenant commanders and lieutenant colonels. Not one genius in the lot. When they came into my office, because somebody had told them they needed a Ph.D., they were convinced they couldn't get a civilian job. Actually, if you're an accountant on a naval base it is not that different from being an accountant anywhere else. But they didn't know it, and they were defeated. I had to talk them into even being willing to be placed. Yet I placed all of them—as business managers of a law firm, for instance, or of an accounting firm, or of a small college. And they came to life again, because they weren't burned out; they were just tired and frightened.

Our institutions are totally unprepared for the second-career need. We will have to learn that what used to be considered the "professions" are essentially careers for older men. In a profession where you're on your own, experience and judgment are far more important than knowledge, whether you are a lawyer, doctor, minister, or teacher. We will come to look upon these as essentially the second-career opportunities for the knowledge worker. But we will also have to make greater mobility possible between institutions.

AN INSTITUTIONALIZED WORLD

Young people sense that our society has become one in which every social task is carried out through a highly organized special-purpose institution: the hospital, the university, the armed services, government agencies, labor unions, research labs, and so on. They see an institutionalized world, and they see right. Their reaction is "Let's tear it down," which isn't going to get them anywhere. The challenge before this generation is not to get rid of institutions, but to make them perform. It's a much tougher challenge. But it is the young who see reality; we older ones see the myth of seventeenth-century political and social theory, in which there is no institution. Society is molecular, and there's only one little organ—the government. Or we see our institution, which is the business enterprise, as the exception in a noninstitutional world. Yet the business enterprise was only the first institution that grew.

Today the world is institutionalized. In the graduate business school at New York University, they used to have only young businessmen in the class. Today they have more and more young executives from other institutions. It reached the point where half of my classes were nonbusiness people. Every mother superior of every Catholic hospital in the city of New York went through that particular class. School principals and hospital superintendents and government people all need management skills.

The multi-institutional world offers personal opportunity. It will enable us to solve the problem of the tired knowledge worker. Many need only a lateral shift. The accountant who moves from a business to a hospital does exactly the same thing, but with a different vocabulary, different values, different relationships. Often it's all he needs to revive. In business we know a little bit about management; that's why they come to us. But management of a business is fairly easy, because we have measurements. A profit and loss account is a measurement in a market economy. It doesn't measure everything, but it measures some things. There is no such measurement in a noneconomic institution. When you work in a hospital you find out that one can't measure anything, if only because there is no objective. There are five thousand conflicting objectives. A government agency is equally difficult. We will have to learn to make management productive for nonbusiness, noneconomic institutions. The best we have in business is crude, unreliable, and controversial, but there is none at all in the hospital, the school, the government agency. Yet they all need management, and the multi-institutional manager is greatly needed.

Let me sum up by saying that I have not really been talking

about individual challenges, but about the fact that there is a new role for the manager. Fifteen years ago one used this statement as a rhetorical way of making the audience feel good. Now it's serious. I am not at all sure that the manager is going to live up to his new role, nor am I sure that it really makes sense. In many ways business management has been the institutional success story of the century. That's why I had the mother superiors in my class. All of us in this room know that management leaves a good deal to be desired. But compared with the other institutions, business management performs and can be measured. By and large we have delivered.

We stand out, and society thinks we can perform. The danger of failure is great, and the social needs of today are big and grim. They require more than managerial ability; many of them require fundamental changes not just in attitudes, but in values. Yet society looks to us to take the leadership, and it holds us responsible not only for the quantities of life but suddenly for the quality of life. Fifteen years ago this new leadership role was nonoperational. It meant taking the lead in the symphony drive, or serving on the college board, where nobody expected to have anything to do except appear at commencement. It didn't mean building a new role into one's performance and one's work. Now it does.

An actor who gets a new role learns lines; he doesn't learn a new role. We all have to learn lines, and I have tried to give you some of them. I talked about individual big jobs; and they're already too big. But they all add up to a change in role—partly because of the visibility and success of management, partly because of the failure of others.

Don't forget, however, that the new role does not absolve us from accountability for the quantities of life. The worst thing we could do today would be to become great social heroes and let the economy collapse. And where do you as an individual manager go to work? Nobody should try to tackle all these areas. You ought to say: "This is what I am going to work on. And for the next five years I'm not even going to listen to anything else." The worst thing you could do is splinter yourself. Nobody can do more than one big job at a time, and few of us can do even one. These are very big jobs.

But if you don't take on one of them, I don't think you are going to achieve. You may get a vice-presidency; one never knows. You may make a career. But I don't think you will feel that you have achieved. And one of the exciting things about this time is that it calls for achievement and contribution on the part of individuals.

SELECTED WRITINGS OF PETER F. DRUCKER

The Age of Discontinuity: Guidelines to Our Changing Society, Harper & Row, New York, 1969.

The Concept of the Corporation, New American Library, New York, 1964. (Paperback.)

The Effective Executive, Harper & Row, 1967.

Management: Tasks, Responsibilities, Practices, Harper & Row, 1974.

Men, Ideas and Politics: Essays, Harper & Row, 1971.

The New Society: The Anatomy of the Industrial Order, Harper & Row, 1962. (Paperback.)

Technology, Management and Society: Essays, Harper & Row, 1970.

THE
ENERGY-ENVIRONMENT
INTERFACE

ॐ

HENRY L. DIAMOND

Henry L. Diamond is executive director of the national Commission on Critical Choices for Americans, a group formed in 1973 by Nelson Rockefeller to study basic decisions facing the country. Among the members are Daniel P. Moynihan, Ivan Allen, Jr., Clarence B. Jones, Daniel J. Boorstin, Carroll L. Wilson, and Bess Myerson. The commission approaches current issues from three premises: that change is taking place more rapidly all the time, that national problems are interrelated, and that national choices must be made not by an elite but by a broad participation of Americans.

Previously Diamond served as commissioner of New York State's Department of Environmental Conservation. A native of Chattanooga, he is a graduate of Vanderbilt and Georgetown Universities and a member of the bars of the U.S. Supreme Court, New York State, Tennessee, and the District of Columbia.

I WOULD like to discuss with you the complex set of relationships between two critical national needs. That fashionable word "interface" is defined as "the place where independent systems meet and act upon or communicate with each other." Applied to the energy-environment situation, the interface is the area where energy and environment priorities collide.

On the one hand, we must produce sufficient energy to keep the country healthy, productive, and secure.

On the other, we must protect the air, water, and land on which life depends.

These purposes clash at a number of points along the interface. One of our major national tasks is to resolve the conflicts and make the two systems interact more smoothly. How well we succeed will go a long way toward determining the quality of American life in the coming years.

My description of the energy-environment interface reflects the work of the Commission on Critical Choices for Americans, which is exploring our interlocked national problems. Let me emphasize, however, that the views expressed here are my own. The conclusions of the entire commission will be issued during 1975.

One of the ideas behind the Commission is that the changes taking place today are accelerating. As a result Americans now have an opportunity to shape the conditions of life not only in the long run for their children, but in the short run for themselves. The energy and environment problems that are now under debate have come into public awareness only recently. Yet by their nature many of them will be settled for better or worse in the immediate future.

During the last decade there was an extraordinary increase in public knowledge about the environmental movement. I would say that the first Earth Day—April 22, 1970—was the time when enthusiasm for environmental issues hit a peak. Before that, ecology had been considered slightly kooky—a bit of a backwater reserved for little old ladies with funny footwear. As a country we realized during the early 1970s that environmental protection was a basic issue. On the strength of its new popularity, the environment won some long-sought victories at the polls and in legislatures. Things started to move.

To be sure, water pollution and air pollution didn't go away and we didn't achieve good land use. Still, we did make a decent environment a national goal backed by a national program and a national policy. The Clean Air Act of 1970 and the Federal Water Pollution Act of 1972 are strong statements of that commitment.

But the smooth sailing for environmental legislation was short-lived. Over the summer and fall of 1973 the crisis in energy swept the environment off the front pages and out of the minds and hearts of legislators. One of the immediate responses in some quarters was to take the energy crisis out on the environment.

For example, a quick way to increase fuel supply is to lift sulfur restrictions on fuel. Sulfur dioxide, a product of burning most fuels, is one of the six major pollutants of the air. Substantial progress was being made in cleaning up this pollutant by severely limiting the amount of sulfur in fuel oil and coal. With the energy crisis came a drive to ease environmental standards so that higher-sulfur fuels could be used, and in some areas it was necessary to grant these variances.

A second interface problem has been offshore oil drilling, which was temporarily stopped on the East Coast by environmentalists who said that the safeguards weren't strict enough. But many people believe that there is substantial energy beneath the ocean waters near major East Coast cities. There will be a strong effort to move ahead on offshore drilling without any more delays, safeguards, or studies.

A third interface problem is strip mining. The easiest and most economic way to mine low-sulfur coal is to strip-mine it in parts of the West and of Kentucky, Ohio, and West Virginia. With the new machinery available, strip mining peels back huge strips of the

surface, leaving swaths of cutaway earth. Unless the land is carefully rehabilitated, it remains a perpetual scar, subject to further
damage by erosion.

A fourth interface conflict will be the use of oil shale. There
may be more oil in the shale in Colorado and Wyoming than there
is in the Middle East's proved reserves, but getting it out means
crunching up a lot of rock and tearing up the countryside in the
process. There will be pressure to accelerate extraction of this oil,
though environmental damage will be extensive without safeguards.

In my opinion the most unfortunate action along the interface
so far has been the decision on the Alaskan pipeline. The merits
could have been debated either way: there will be an adverse impact on the environment, yet we badly need Alaska's reserves. The
disturbing fact is that the usual processes were short-circuited by
direct action of Congress. In effect, the lawmakers said, "Because
of the peculiar problem here, we will disregard what we legislated
in the National Environmental Policy Act of 1969." Whatever the
merits of the case, the gutting of the process was ominous.

These are the problems of interaction along the energy-environment interface, and in spite of their difficulty they are the kind of
problems that we can meet and solve. There will be some short-
term environmental setbacks, but in the long run I am optimistic
about the effect of the energy crisis on the environment. Indeed, if
we are very, very shrewd and manage our affairs well, the energy
crisis can be a plus for the environment.

There are two reasons why I believe that energy and environment are not implacable enemies—that in fact they can be allies.
One is that the conservation ethic has been renewed by the energy
crisis. The conservation program, a somewhat forgotten part of the
environmental movement, is based on the principle that we should
avoid waste and consume only what is necessary. In our affluent
society, particularly with our assumption that energy was almost
free, we lost sight of that principle even as we were raising our

environmental consciousness. We were wasteful while we preached ecology.

Asking the public to cut down on its consumption of energy was surprisingly successful. Certainly while the crisis was at its peak, people did use less gasoline and less electricity—in fact, so much less electricity that some utilities had to seek a rate increase because of reduced consumption.

If the effort to save energy is to show substantial results, however, there must be more basic changes and more basic commitment than can be made by private consumers alone. Industry, which uses about 40 percent of our total energy, must play a major role. Readily available measures which do not require process changes or additional capital investment can produce energy savings of 10 to 15 percent. Beyond that, long-term investment is needed to make some basic alterations.

As part of the long-range goal I believe there will be an emphasis on lighter-weight automobiles. Gas consumption is directly related to auto weight, so that if the average weight per car is 2,500 pounds rather than 5,000 pounds, there is almost a 50 percent reduction in fuel use.

In reality the conservation effort can help both the energy and the environment crises. It is a simplification but a true one to say that the air pollution problem is basically a function of what is burned. If we burn less, there is less pollution. In places like the New York metropolitan area, the automobile is probably responsible for 95 percent of the carbon monoxide in the air. The key factor is vehicle miles traveled. If this figure is reduced, carbon monoxide and hydrocarbon levels go down. And that is exactly what has happened with the energy crisis. Although we don't have the figures yet to prove it, gasoline consumption figures lead us to believe that less carbon monoxide and less hydrocarbons are going into the air.

The second reason for my optimism is that the energy crisis is challenging the capabilities of American research and development genius. The scarcity of oil and its high price will bring other processes on the line which had previously been ignored because they were difficult or expensive. I believe that in developing these new technologies, we are ready to accept the principle that they must be environmentally sound.

Thus if offshore drilling is to take place, we must develop more safeguards for the environment. In the case of oil shale, we are really starting with a clean slate in production processes. We should be able to build environmental safeguards into the technology of extraction.

The coal situation holds similar opportunities. Seven or eight years ago we decided that if we were going to clean up the air, the easiest and best way to do it was with low-sulfur oil. We knew that we had a several-hundred-year supply of coal, and that it was technically possible to clean it by taking out the sulfur and extracting the particulate matter either before burning or after. But because oil was then $2 a barrel, it was easier and cheaper to burn it instead of cleaning up the coal. We did not put our investment into research and development of such techniques as stack gas cleaning or liquefaction and gasification. We made a great effort to switch coal-burning plants to oil by means of statutes and local ordinances. With oil above $10 a barrel, however, coal becomes much more attractive, even with the added costs to clean it.

If we can work out the technology to clean up coal, and if we can create a climate where long-term investment in coal is attractive, the potential is tremendous. Only 19 percent of our present energy comes from coal. If it could be doubled—and it could— we could wipe out our dependence on imported oil.

Technology applied to the energy problem can bring us other direct environmental benefits. In New York City, for example, 26 million tons of garbage are generated every day. Some cities are already experimenting with burning garbage as a source of energy, because it contains roughly the BTU value of low-grade coal. It is hard to handle and its use requires an adjustment of boilers, but with oil at current prices garbage becomes much more attractive. Consolidated Edison will probably be burning solid waste from New York City at its Arthur Kill plant very soon.

Once we thought we had a solid-waste crisis. It was often noted that each person in the New York City area produces $5\frac{1}{2}$ to 6 pounds of solid waste a day. With the technology now available right off the shelf, $5\frac{1}{2}$ pounds of solid waste would generate 1 kilowatt of electricity. If steps were taken to convert the waste to gas or to oil, it would satisfy about 10 percent of our total electrical needs. So in this case, what was considered an environmental crisis may turn out to be an asset as we find solutions to the energy crisis.

Let me return to the definition of interface: "The place at which independent systems meet and act upon or communicate with each other." Let's emphasize that word "communicate," because it may be part of the problem in energy-environment conflicts.

On the one hand, the people charged with or primarily interested in assuring energy supplies have urged the repeal of some hard-won environmental victories. Joining them are factions who never wanted the environmental effort to succeed in the first place. These groups have fought for repeal of the Clean Air Act. They have opposed any limits on strip mining, and they have urged rapid acceleration of offshore drilling and oil shale production without proper environmental safeguards.

Their campaigns have been opposed by environmentalists and others. Unfortunately, a few members of the environmental movement have adopted an absolute "Never—not an inch!" attitude. It is true that some of the new legislation and regulations are onerous. Perhaps there are some provisions of the Federal Water Pollution Control Act and the Clean Air Act of 1970 which deserve criticism. But for a small number of environmentalists to take an unyielding stand may in the long run be self-defeating. The country will continue to operate in something like the life-style to which we are accustomed, and it will require increased energy to do so. The challenge is to work out the communications and other problems along the interface for the greatest good.

I believe there is enormous potential for doing so. Energy and the environment are inexorably interlocked, for better or worse. Because each has something it can give the other, I am convinced that their interaction can be for the better. Environment offers the energy crisis its conservation ethic, so that by citizen action and by some basic changes in the way we do things, we can slow down the growth in energy demand. Just how much this growth can be retarded is debatable, but it's clear that an investment in conservation will bring about reduced demand curves.

Conversely, energy can offer the environmental crisis the opportunity for sophisticated technological solutions which have been overlooked or considered too expensive. The technical fixes that high oil prices and new research efforts are creating may show us alternate paths to a clean environment. Too often, environmentalists have regarded all technical development with disdain and have sought only the simple solutions of "less." Here is an opportunity to create a "more" in an environmentally sound way.

Thus we may find that the critical choice of the energy-environment interface is not and should not be a choice between one or the other. Rather, it is a series of innovative decisions, so that the strengths of one can help solve the needs of the other. That's what successful interfacing is all about.

QUESTIONS AND ANSWERS

Do you believe that one of the critical issues facing both corporations and individuals in the United States is the rate of no growth?

This is a popular debate right now. But the feeling I get from talking with the commission members is that it isn't a growth–no-growth situation so much as a question of a shift in growth. Some people argue that we ought to shift some of our growth out of hardware and into education or medical services, and I see this as the emerging issue. I don't think the country's going to quit growing.

Is anything being done to develop the coal industry—to facilitate its expansion by improving mine safety, mechanization, and so on?

A lot of thought is being given to it, and there will probably be some federal legislation as the price of coal becomes attractive and people become willing to make long-term commitments. Granting more favorable freight rates for coal is one possibility. As with the oil industry, depletion allowances will probably have to be created. It's a complicated situation, because it is difficult to judge how eager the oil companies are to bring their competitors on. The coal business was depressed, and the oil companies, which then became the primary energy suppliers, made heavy investments in plant and equipment. But stimulation for the coal industry is likely to come out of Congress.

Isn't the energy crisis partly due to the fact that we've had a deliberate, regulated policy of cheap energy? The electric industry has certainly been regulated in a way to force the price of energy down and keep it to a minimum. The Tennessee Valley Authority didn't just happen! Why not the oil companies?

I think that the New Deal probably did a lot of good at the time and provided one of the major solutions to our social problems regarding energy. Everybody needed access to cheap energy, so it became a high point of political and social policy to ensure it. Today we are reaping the economic consequences of that policy. Prices are artificial, just as natural gas prices are. The price of natural gas has been artificially kept so low that it discouraged new development. This has helped to ruin the coal industry, and by encouraging low import quotas as another way of keeping prices low, it has exported some of our problems overseas.

Yes, I think you're right in saying that the oil crisis is in many ways the product of our own policies—our own critical choices of the 1930s. Inverted rate structures have encouraged energy waste by charging less per added kilowatt, when it should probably be the other way around.

Other sources of energy besides coal, oil, and natural gas are hydroelectric and atomic energy. We don't hear much about the need to spend money in these areas—yet it could change our dependence.

Hydro is now 4 percent of the total electric generation in this country, and there are not many good sites left. So with the exception of pumped storage plants, the hydro potential is limited.

Nuclear energy is less than 1 percent of the total energy. I was amazed to find that we get more energy from burning wood than we do from nuclear power. In the early 1950s we thought that nuclear power was going to solve all our problems, but today we find that it hasn't worked very well. For example, in New York, Indian Point No. 1 and Indian Point No. 2 have a lot of operating problems. Many of them are blamed on the environmentalists—somewhat unfairly, in my view, because the darned things just don't seem to work very well. Maybe they will eventually; there are thousands of nuclear plants on the drawing boards.

How about thermal energy?

That is an exotic and limited project, because you've got to be in an area where there is some water which will generate energy. It's a useful supplementary source of energy, but not a big solution.

The most attractive solution in terms of availability and cost seems to be solar energy. If you get the sunshine, you can solve the storage problems. In the Southern tier of this country, and in other parts of the world that have a lot of sunshine, the practicalities of solar energy become very real.

Federal regulation has a poor track record. If there is regulation, how do you propose to stimulate an industry?

This is one of the basic choices the country faces, because the federally regulated industries haven't been too successful. Probably the outstanding examples are the railroads and the airlines. They started out as vigorous, young growth industries with a lot of investor interest. Now, they're in the doldrums. Excess regulation has killed the railroads, and today we find out that we need them badly.

Have the panels of your commission looked down the road to see what our long-term problems are? For example, how are we going to supply the food for generations to come?

Yes, we've been looking down the road. Two themes have emerged: one focused on issues like food, the second on Americans' malaise and dissatisfaction with their institutions—lack of confidence in government, big corporations, unions, churches. The campus unrest of the middle 1960s seems to have quieted down, but it may have been replaced by indifference and apathy resembling that of the 1950s, which is just as serious a problem.

A number of modern industrial nations have overcome severe obstacles. Is there nothing we can learn from them? Are our problems so unique that we have to solve them all by ourselves?

You've made a very good point which we as a country sometimes overlook. Our problems are not unique, and our solutions are not necessarily the best available. Our people have been better housed and fed than people in most countries, but they have not been provided with better medical services. I suspect that the quality of mass medical care in the United States ranks forty-first, right after Senegal. Yes, there are things that we ought to learn from other nations. We're experimenting with some of them. I think we are much more receptive now than we used to be.

Will the energy crisis be worse for other cities than for New York?

Yes, in some ways New York is fortunate with regard to the energy crisis. Although our rapid transit system is not ideal, it makes us better off than, say, Los Angeles, which doesn't have one. Perhaps a side effect of the energy crisis may be that people return to the central cities and rediscover the conveniences of urban life.

We've spent billions of dollars to go to the moon and bring back a handful of rocks. Don't you think that we could have used the money to devise different transportation systems, to provide assistance for cities like Los Angeles, to improve our educational system, to lessen our tax burdens, and so on?

I think that's very true. If we had put the effort which we used in going to the moon toward environment, housing, or schools, we would have solved many of our problems. Unfortunately, priorities are not set in a nice, clean commission room but in Congress and the state legislatures. That's where we have to make our national choices known.

How is the Commission on Critical Choices funded?

We have a total budget of about 6.5 million dollars, and the start-up grant from Nelson and Laurance Rockefeller was 2 million dollars. Contributions and pledges have come from a large number of individuals and from foundations that support public-interest activities.

How can the Commission on Critical Choices be a viable force in effecting change?

I think that good ideas take hold. Also, the members of the commission, many of whom are leaders of Congress, are in a position to help implement them. I have often been asked whether the commission is a political vehicle. The answer is no; the commission's membership is bipartisan, and our recommendations will be available to all candidates.

My belief is that if we develop good ideas and inject them into the public debate in 1976—if we get the public and the politicians talking about the right issues—we will be doing a service. Out there somewhere I think there's a longing for leadership, for some kind of direction, after the turmoil of Vietnam and Watergate. We'll see; I'm betting several years of my life on it.

THE
CHANGING
REGULATORY
SCENE

❧

CARL E. BAGGE

Carl E. Bagge served as a Republican member of the Federal Power Commission from 1965 to 1970. At the end of his five-year term he became president of the National Coal Association, which represents coal operators and allied industries in Washington. During his period with the FPC, Bagge was chairman of the interdepartmental Working Committee on Utilities of the President's Council on Recreation and Natural Beauty. This committee produced the first environmental study of the country's utility industries.

A native of Chicago, Bagge received his training at Augustana College in Illinois, Uppsala University in Sweden, the University of Southern California, and Northwestern University. Before he joined the FPC he was general attorney for the Atchison, Topeka, and Santa Fe Railroad.

TODAY in this unprecedented era of change, people are developing new values, making new demands, and challenging policies in every part of government. Regulatory agencies are being subjected to pressures that are just as powerful as the economic forces which first led to the establishment of regulation. Federal and state regulatory dockets now include such subjects as air and water pollution, hiring practices, esthetic standards, customer deposit practices, and undergrounding policies. And regulators are coming to realize that their methodology is sometimes incapable of coping with these new issues. Indeed, today the issues often transcend the capacities of traditional regulation and the administrative process.

To respond to society's new demands, regulatory agencies need a new philosophy that departs from the limited goals and adversary philosophy of the past. First, however, it is necessary to understand the nature of the goals that society has adopted and the shortcomings of traditional methodology in dealing with them. In thinking about recent developments in the regulatory field, I have found it helpful to divide them into three categories: institutional, substantive, and procedural.

INSTITUTIONAL DEVELOPMENTS

As an institution, the regulatory process is being reshaped by new political pressures and by structural changes in the regulated industries themselves. Politically the consumer movement, the environmental ethic, the drive toward participatory politics, the demand for freedom of information, and the urban crisis all are pushing the regulatory agencies to adopt objectives that were regarded as irrelevant a few years ago. Structurally the regulated industries have accommodated to new technology and expanded from local to regionwide units. In the process they have outgrown their regulatory machinery.

CONSUMERISM AND ENVIRONMENTALISM   These two political movements have already led us as a nation to make regulatory decisions that would have been unthinkable in the past. Unfortunately, many decisions with an environmental orientation have added substantially to consumer costs.

The environmental ethic is the most compelling factor in the changing institutional role of regulation. Before it gained power, our society had encouraged quantity for the sake of quantity, growth for the sake of growth, technology for technology's sake. Even today there are people who retain this misdirected cornucopian viewpoint, but they have lost influence. Americans have come to understand that human values must be preserved and that growth must be channeled to accommodate them.

In my opinion, the environmental movement first surfaced as a national issue in 1965, when Stanford University wanted to attach its nuclear accelerator to a generating plant west of the coastal range in California. The residents of the nearby town of Woodside refused to permit construction of the transmission facilities because the lines would be visible where they crossed the mountains. In a political compromise worked out under the direction of Laurance Rockefeller, the lines were set low enough to be inconspicuous in the forested mountain areas.

Ten years ago environmentalism was a benign political movement; today it is something less than benign. It has been transformed into a zealous faith and a national priority. I base this observation on my experience as a member of the Federal Power Commission and as chairman of the Working Committee on Utilities of the President's Council on Recreation and National Beauty. Today there is no decision that can be made by any regulatory agency without considering its possible impact upon esthetics and the environment.

PARTICIPATORY POLITICS   The public concern for environmental values coexists with an unprecedented public demand for participation in utility and regulatory decision making. Bills have been introduced repeatedly in Congress to establish consumers' and environmental counsels' rights to intervene in all regulatory agencies. Regulatory hearings today would hardly be complete without their demonstrators—angry people who, by their physical presence, voice opposition to the routing of utility lines and the choice of sites for generating stations.

Citizens picket on behalf of all sorts of programs—consumerism and environmentalism among them—and all sorts of policies, such as nondiscriminatory hiring. The FPC, for example, is responsible for licensing nonfederal hydroelectric projects, and in a license proceeding a few years ago the allegation was made that Pacific Gas & Electric's hiring practices were not consistent with the federal Civil Rights Act. Passing judgment on issues like these is a new experience for the regulatory agencies.

FREEDOM OF INFORMATION   The movement for freedom of information has been reflected in federal legislation aimed at exposing large parts of the regulatory decision-making process. I agree with this principle, except when the communication involved is between the commissioners and members of the agency's staff. Exposing these interchanges to public view seriously hampers the free expression of ideas. A few years ago the Second Circuit refused to extend the scope of the Freedom of Information Act to communications between the FPC and its staff, a decision for which I am grateful. But aside from staff interchanges, I believe that giving the maximum exposure to all lines of communication helps maintain the integrity of decision making.

URBAN CRISIS   The political pressures generated by the urban crisis come to a focus in the area of rate making. One new demand is that regulatory commissions raise unit rates to the larger users in order to restrict growth in the consumption of electric power. Another demand challenges the traditional view of non-discrimination in utility rate making. An example is the proposal that metropolitan transit rates be reduced in the inner city in order to achieve social goals. This concept is now being pressed in urban transit cases and electric utility rate regulation. The advocates contend that the idea of nondiscrimination—which had been bedrock in utility rate regulation—is no longer relevant.

GOVERNMENT RESPONSE Legislative and administrative proposals have proliferated in response to political criticism of the regulatory agencies. Federal legislation—such as the Metcalf bill, S 607, the Kennedy environmental bill, S 1071, and the action of the Administrative Conference of the United States concerning the establishment of a people's counsel—is a direct response to these trends. The ICC Reorganization Plan and HR 12068 provided explicitly for the appointment of the chairman of two of the major agencies by the President. Those proposals reflect a desire to make the independent agencies more responsive to executive policy making. Bill HR 8017 proposing to create a Congressional ombudsman (similar to the Parliamentary Commissioner for Administration enacted by the English Parliament in 1967) was an effort to make the independent agencies more responsive to political currents. The Ash Commission's recommendations to abolish the collegial form of decision making except for the FCC was another attempt to alter the institutional character of the regulatory process.

Other legislation has also affected the nature of the regulatory process. In recent years Congress has passed the Automobile Safety Act, the Flammable Products Act, the Federal Meat Inspection Act, the Water Quality Act, the Air Quality Act, and the Pipeline Safety Act. Such laws have effectively extended government regulation of business outside the traditional apparatus of independent regulatory agencies. Regulation by the establishment of minimum standards may become even more widespread in the future as government seeks a more flexible and responsive apparatus to cope with contemporary problems.

Analysis of all this government activity indicates that we have two basic alternatives. We can strengthen the existing agencies and reshape their administrative methodology to enable them to become responsive to changing goals. Or we can diffuse regulatory responsibility by creating separately administered standards and ancillary organizations which could intervene on behalf of their special responsibilities: say, the environment, consumers, or the poor. The second alternative would make the administrative process more adversary in nature and cumbersome in operation. Within the agencies, it would encourage development of a tradition-bound mentality eager to defend the status quo.

The temptation is to formulate short-term solutions to problems by superimposing additional adversary parties to represent each new interest. But the essential shortcoming of the regulatory process today is its methodology—the requirement that every aspect of a proposal be subjected to adversary hearings and tested in the crucible of due process. Creating additional adversary bodies will only compound the difficulties.

What we need is a significant departure from adversary proceedings. We need to create machinery for consultation and joint planning, machinery which can accommodate new interests as they arise, so that they can participate fully in regulatory decisions. In addition, the administrative agencies urgently need adequate budgets for hiring and developing a professional corps of personnel. State agencies need federal money, federal loans of expert personnel, and closer relations with federal agencies in the form of joint boards.

STRUCTURAL CHANGES IN REGULATED INDUSTRIES
Structural changes have taken place in all the regulated industries. Their direction can be seen in the electric utility industry, which

in the past fifteen years has grown from a predominantly local into a regionally coordinated operation. As a result the utilities need regional regulation rather than regulation by states. Joint planning and joint participation in the construction of massive generating units, in order to achieve economies of scale and to take advantage of seasonal diversity, require joint regulation. The new technology has posed monumental environmental problems which the regulatory apparatus must cope with.

In several instances, state commissions have joined forces to deal with problems regionally. Following the 1967 blackout, for example, the PJM regional power pool was created by the utility commissions of Pennsylvania, Maryland, New Jersey, and the District of Columbia. The concerns of this group were extended to environmental considerations in the Calvert Cliffs nuclear licensing proceeding. The regional regulatory concept exists in another form under the Southern Governors' Conference, where state utility commissions work jointly on issues of thermal pollution, nuclear radiation, and air pollution with a regional compact—the Southern Interstate Nuclear Board.

The eleven Western states now participate jointly not only among their commissions, but with the regional reliability council in reliability planning and in planning generating station sites and transmission corridors. Southern California Edison and Pacific Gas & Electric, for example, have a profound effect upon the entire utility industry in the West. The Western states today are interconnected in one massive system under the Pacific Northwest-Southwest intertie, in which hydropower from the Northwest is transmitted by a DC line to the southern California market. Because of environmental opposition, Southern California Edison has been unable to build enough generating stations and therefore has a real need for this power.

With the construction of the West Coast Intertie, for technological reasons of system stability it has become necessary to construct a corresponding transmission facility west of the Rocky

Mountains to complete a regional "loop." This has created a unique regulatory problem. A less populated state such as Utah is required to place into its rate base a substantial investment for protecting the integrity of the backbone electric power transmission capacity for all eleven Western states. Yet Utah consumers are otherwise adequately served by the existing facilities of Utah Power and Light. The Western state regulatory commissions are working with the Western regional reliability council to try and solve the kind of regulatory problem posed by the construction of the loop through Utah. In this way, structural changes in a regulated industry have led to a broad response by regulators which is profoundly influencing the institution of regulation.

In addition, the regulatory process itself is being extended beyond the scope of the independent regulatory agency. In planning transmission corridors and generating sites, for example, the electric utility industry is increasingly working with local and regional government planning agencies. State utility commissions are extending their certification jurisdiction over these facilities. Perhaps eventually the commissions will be able to make long-range plans with all interested parties well in advance of the certification process. Environmental problems could then be resolved in time to meet tomorrow's power needs.

SUBSTANTIVE DEVELOPMENTS

The original purpose of the independent regulatory agencies was to protect the citizen in his role as a consumer, a purchaser of goods and services—an economic man. Thus the concept of the public interest as it was forged in the statutes establishing the agencies was directed toward an economic goal—prices, rates, and charges.

ECOLOGIC MAN   But in the decades since the agencies were founded, a new role has emerged for them. Economic man is still important, but our concerns today are wider and deeper. The environmental ethic encompasses man in relation to his total environment, against the background of an increasingly complex, urbanized, and interdependent society. It can be said that our regulatory concerns extend beyond economic man to ecologic man. The sooner we define our new goals in each area of regulatory oversight, the sooner we can take action to achieve them.

We can no longer even think about our problems in the framework of the past. For example, transportation policy cannot be formulated in terms of conflicts between maritime policy, surface transport policy, highway construction programs, and air transport policies. The transportation crisis must be approached in an integrated mobile urban society. And so it is in every other area of government regulation.

QUALITY OF LIFE Regulators, both state and federal, are obliged to reassess their policies in relation to the new national goal of preserving and enhancing the quality of life. This goal has given rise to a wide range of entirely new issues before the regulatory agencies. The public's concern with the quality of broadcasting is the most fundamental issue before the Federal Communications Commission. The public's concern with the quality of merchandise lies at the heart of the issues before the Federal Trade Commission. The public's concern with the integrity and quality of electric power service is dominant at the Federal Power Commission. The public's concern with the quality of transportation service is the major issue at the Interstate Commerce Commission. In demanding higher quality in products and services, the public also insists that it be achieved without impairing the quality of the environment. Hence fundamental questions are being raised today about the efficacy of such basic technology as the internal combustion engine, central-station power generation, and overhead power transmission.

All the substantive issues in these areas share a common concern for the quality of life. The greatest challenge to the regulatory process is whether it is sufficiently flexible and creative to respond to this new cluster of public values.

PROCEDURAL DEVELOPMENTS

Just as the goals of regulation have been extended beyond the limited economic objectives of the past, so a new regulatory methodology is required for dealing with the broad problems that do not lend themselves to the adversary approach. Rational regulatory policy cannot be forged in bits and pieces chosen by a few interested parties. A formalized consultative process between government and business is needed for joint planning and joint action, for rule making in place of adjudication, and for investigatory proceedings. We also need joint action between government agencies, both federal and state, which share responsibility for the same sectors of the economy.

Regulation as we have known it in the past will be increasingly displaced by cooperative efforts based upon a mature relationship between government and industry, and between federal and state governments. This is already apparent in many areas. In the FPC, for example, the new approach can be seen in the National Power Survey, the National Gas Survey, the commission's work on the problem of electric power reliability, and its approach to offshore gas transmission facilities in south Louisiana. All these are problems which require regulatory oversight but simply do not lend themselves to traditional methodology.

CONCLUSION

The new public concern for the quality of life calls for a new regulatory philosophy that departs from the limited goals and adversary methodology of the past. But recent proposals in Congress and in the Administrative Conference of the United States would extend these adversary perimeters and perpetuate the goals of the past that focus on economic man. Regulation today is at a crossroads. If it is to discharge its new responsibilities, the regulatory process must be made relevant to our national goals. This can be achieved within the existing regulatory structure by giving primary emphasis to joint planning by means of the consultative process. With a broader regulatory philosophy, recognition of the expanded goals of regulation, and the creation of a procedural methodology capable of dealing with the new goals, regulation can meet the challenge provided by our concern for the quality of life.

SELECTED WRITINGS OF CARL E. BAGGE

"Affluence and Effluents: The Challenge of Environment Quality Control," *Public Utilities Fortnightly,* April 27, 1967.

"Broadening the Supply Base: A Proposal to Eliminate Producer Price Regulation," *Natural Resources Lawyer,* July 1970.

"Coal: An Overlooked Energy Source" (1972 Gabrielson Lecture, Colby College), *Vital Speeches of the Day,* April 1, 1972.

"Coal and the Environment," *Natural Resources Lawyer* (Journal of the Section of Natural Resources Law, American Bar Association), January 1972.

"Coal: The Energy Key to World Stability (Address to 10th Biennial Meeting, Council of the Association for Coal in Europe, St. Ives, England), *Vital Speeches of the Day,* July 1, 1973.

"A Decade of FPC Regulation," *Boston College Industrial and Commercial Law Review,* May 1970.

"The Federal Power Commission and Freedom of Information," *Administrative Law Review,* American Bar Association, March 1971.

"Gas Producer Price Legislation: An Alternative to Whistling in the Dark," *Natural Resources Lawyer*, January 1971.

"Liquefied Natural Gas Imports and the United States Energy Crisis: A Regulatory Response," *Law & Policy in International Business*, 1972.

"North American Energy Self-Sufficiency" (Address to 26th Annual Canadian Conference on Coal, Calgary, Alberta), *Vital Speeches of the Day*, Nov. 1, 1974.

"The Potential of Coal to Meet the Energy Crisis," *Energy Systems and Policy*, Fall 1974.

"The Quality of Life: Challenge to Regulation," *Public Utilities Fortnightly*, Sept. 10, 1970.

"Reflections of a Coal Man," *Vital Speeches of the Day*, Jan. 1, 1973.

"Should Prosecutors Write Agency Opinions? The Role of Agency Counsel in Decision Making," *Administrative Law Review*, June 1970.

"There's Coal in Oil's Future" (Address to Annual Meeting, National Petroleum Refiners Association, Miami), *Vital Speeches of the Day*, May 15, 1974.

SETTLEMENT
GEOGRAPHY
AND
TELECOMMUNICATIONS
The Next Twenty Years

❧

RONALD ABLER

Ronald Abler, associate professor of geography at The Pennsylvania State University, is a specialist in communications media and their relation to settlement patterns. From 1972 to 1974 he served as associate director and atlas editor of a comprehensive study of the twenty largest metropolitan systems in the United States. Currently he is working on a book about the geography of communications.

Abler was born in 1939 in Milwaukee and took his undergraduate and graduate degrees at the University of Minnesota. He has been a visiting professor of geography there and at the University of British Columbia.

I WANT to talk today about some potential social and economic effects of telecommunications technology, broadly conceived. I'll say something about the current settlement geography of the United States, place it in a historical context, and suggest some relationships between settlement patterns and telecommunications over the next twenty years.

CONCENTRATION IN CITIES

The amount of land and the number of people in the United States would be judged about right by world standards. In 1970 we had approximately $3\frac{1}{2}$ million square miles of land and 203 million people. This works out to about 6 percent of the world's population and 6 percent of the world's land area, and represents an overall density of around 57 people per square mile.

Yet as the diagram shows, land use in the United States is quite uneven. Virtually every part of the nation is inhabited, although at densities well below 10 people per square mile in the mountains and intermontane areas of the West. But population is heavily concentrated in large metropolitan areas.

In fact, 68 percent of us have chosen to live in standard metropolitan statistical areas. These consist of counties in or adjacent to large cities, and many contain considerable open land. Urbanized (continuously built-up) areas amount to only 1 percent of our national space—but they are homes for 58 percent of the people. This is a startling degree of concentration. If the entire population of the country were to occupy land at similar densities, all 203 million people could easily live in the state of Pennsylvania.

FOUR SETTLEMENT ERAS

Our urban concentration is unprecedented in human history. How did it come about? And more important, does the story of its development offer any clues to the future?

Area and Population of the United States, 1970
3,537,000 square miles
203,212,000 people

Nonmetropolitan Areas
3,149,000 square miles (90%)
63,794,000 people (32%)

Metropolitan Areas
388,000 square miles (10%)
139,418,000 people (68%)

Urbanized (built-up) Areas
35,000 square miles (1%)
118,447,000 people (58%)

Throughout time the two major determinants of settlement patterns have been the population's dominant economic activity and dominant transportation technology. They have governed the choice of locations for large cities and the evolution of their internal organization. By examining production systems and transportation technology, we can identify four settlement eras in the United States: an agricultural era, a manufacturing era, a service era, and a communications era.

SETTLEMENT ERAS IN THE UNITED STATES

	Agricultural (To 1850)	Manufacturing (1850–1920)	Service (1920–1960)	Communications (1960–?)
Key resource	Land	Materials	People	Information
Transportation	Foot/Horse	Water/Rail	Auto/Air	Telecommunications
Settlement pattern	Dispersed	City	Metropolis	Dispersed?

The agrarian era in the United States lasted until about 1850. The major transportation technologies were foot and horse, with some water transportation. The major resource was land, and settlement was dispersed in order to exploit the land resource. Population was scattered over the landscape and cities were the tip of the population iceberg.

As the economy shifted to manufacturing in the 1850s, the second era began. The movement technology of importance was water transportation, and a little later on, rail. The resources that people used to make money were raw materials and power. Thus cities began to develop at water-power sites and at places where raw materials could be assembled for the production of goods. Although cities were important before then, manufacturing provided the real push for modern urbanism at power and assembly sites.

The third settlement era in the United States was the service period. An increasing fraction of the labor force earned its living by doing things for other people. This period stretched from roughly 1920 to 1960. In the service era, the important resources are people. When you walk into a service establishment such as a barbershop, you're the raw material; when you walk out, you're the finished product. The transport bases in this period are the auto and the freeway. A society dependent on services must have a settlement pattern that gives people access to many other people. The settlement pattern that evolves in the service period is the metropolis—the giant city that bursts the bonds of the traditional city and spills over for miles and miles into the countryside.

Since 1960, new ways of producing wealth have become prominent. Information-handling activities are booming, and the office building is becoming the characteristic metropolitan employment center. Cities now compete for office activities in the same way they used to compete for manufacturing plants. Information is the dominant resource; we make money by gathering information, manipulating it in various ways, and acting upon it. The transportation medium of importance is telecommunications, and there is a great deal of speculation that we are on the threshold of a new settlement era that will be a sharp break with the past.

SETTLEMENT AND TELECOMMUNICATIONS

In considering settlement and communications over the next twenty years, let's examine first the vision—what the experts think could happen—and then the realities—the obstacles to attainment of the vision.

VISION: DISPERSAL As I've suggested, the vision is a fourth settlement era in which telecommunications replaces transportation. Information is the major resource, but telecommunications makes information available everywhere, rendering cities and metropolitan centers obsolete. Population will disperse, and we will gradually abandon places like Manhattan and central Chicago as employment migrates to metropolitan peripheries and exurban areas.

The vision is plausible. Further dispersal would continue a local trend that has been operating for well over a century. Even the pre-industrial city had carriage districts where the wealthy resided at some distance from their places of employment. The industrial city and railway transportation spawned the railway suburb, where the wealthy could build large houses on large lots. Dispersal continued in the late 1920s and accelerated in the post–World War II period, because the democratization of individual transportation in the form of automobiles and freeways enabled the bulk of the population to enjoy mobility too.

Contrary to popular opinion, population density in our cities has decreased over the last century. Up until about 1830, city densities were typically well over 20,000 people per square mile. In parts of Manhattan and other cities that had large influxes of immigrants, densities sometimes went as high as 200,000 or 300,000 per square mile. With horse trolleys, and with the application of rail transportation in the form of the electric trolley, people spread out. Between 1870 and 1920 urban settlement was at densities that averaged 10,000 people per square mile. From 1920 to 1960 we experienced a third era of metropolitan settlement with densities that average about 6,000 people per square mile. Thus there has been a continuous decline in urban population densities over the last 150 years.

The historical trend toward lower density continued between 1960 and 1970. If we focus again on the part of the United States that is continuously built up, it amounted to about 25,000 square miles in 1960 and 35,000 square miles in 1970. With a population increase in urbanized areas from 96 million in 1960 to

118 million in 1970, we experienced a density decrease. Urbanized-area population density dropped from 3,900 people per square mile in 1960 to 3,400 people per square mile in 1970.

Continued dispersal would be in harmony with long-term trends, and there is widespread belief that dispersal will and should continue. People concerned with urban pathologies tend to reject the city as a viable settlement pattern. They argue that we should use electronic communications media and the information economy to annihilate distance. They want to extend settlement at the periphery and to create a dispersed metropolitan fabric knit together by electronic communications. Many hope that we can use our electronic communications technology to solve our settlement problems—to get away from the bizarre situation in which 60 percent of the people live on 1 percent of the land.

Most of these visions are based on an audiovisual complex that in turn is based on cable television. The October 1973 issue of *The Futurist,* for example, said: "Cable communications can permit the population of our overcrowded cities to disperse. It will enable those who remain to form cohesive communities with easy and effective access to each other."

Many people talk about the wired city, the wired nation, or even the wired world. And when enthusiasts start describing these technologies and their relations to settlement patterns, the vision is very attractive.

Nicholas Johnson wrote in his book *How to Talk Back to Your Television Set:* "The ultimate vision is a home communications center where a person works, learns and is entertained and contributes to his society by way of communication techniques we have not yet imagined—incidentally solving our commuter traffic jams and much of the air pollution problem in the process."

Brian Berry, the dean of American urban geographers, argues: "The essence of the change is that we are moving into an era of telemobility and from mechanical into electronic environments . . . the revolutionary aspect of electronic environments is not that they reduce the frictions of moving goods and people, but that they move the experience itself to the human nervous system."

John R. Pierce: "We no longer need to live in the heart of the city to meet other people, to use rare facilities, or to see or participate in rare events. I believe that in the future, improved communication will enable us to avoid much onerous travel. We can live where we like, travel for pleasure and communicate to work."

Edward E. David: "Communication technology and computers provide a means for overcoming the tyranny of geography by allowing us to create communities of interest independent of geographical groupings."

The notion is clear: electronic communications is ultramobility. It will make all previous kinds of mobility obsolete. We can have a dispersal of employment, and because it's clear that people follow economic opportunities—and because it's also clear that within the limits imposed by the necessity to make a living, people in the United States prefer to live at low densities—dispersed settlement will result.

Dispersal, then, is an atractive option. The visions are luscious, and may even be accurate in the long run. I certainly think these visions are settlement options that we don't want to foreclose, even though there might be some problems involved in attaining the conditions that are described.

REALITIES   But now let's consider the realities of the situation. Between our current circumstances and the visions of dispersal are a number of obstacles, some of them formidable.

HARDWARE   Let's talk first about hardware. I'm not an engineer, but it seems to me that hardware is probably the least of our worries. I don't mean to say that it's negligible, since most of the visions implicitly assume a random-access color network with full two-way capability and ancillary conveniences such as facsimile services and access to computers.

We do have much of this hardware in the labs, and the purely technical problems are to some extent solved. But bringing it out of the labs will be much more difficult than producing the prototypes. And I suspect it may be more difficult in video communications than it has been with previous communications technologies. I understand that video switching is far more demanding than voice grade switching. It's going to be a while before we solve the problems of providing a switching plant that's capable of doing the same thing for video transmission that our voice-switching network does.

I don't want to shove technical and hardware difficulties under the rug. At the same time, I really think they're the least serious obstacles to attaining our visions; economic problems will probably turn out to be much worse than the hardware problems.

CAPITAL INVESTMENT   A large percentage of our private investment is now going into the voice communications plant. Over the last three or four years about one-twelfth of American investment in new plant and equipment was channeled into communications. As the graph shows, in 1970 we allocated approximately 10 billion dollars to telecommunications out of a total private investment of 80 billion.

So the voice network is already using a large amount of our capital. But when we project a national video network, we're talking about money on a different scale altogether. There are many estimates of the cost of such a plant. A fairly reasonable opinion is that we could build one similar to the kind described in futurist visions for about a trillion dollars.

This is an interesting number, because a trillion dollars was our 1971 gross national product—the value of all goods and services produced in the United States during that year. How long might it be before the country will be able to make a comparable investment in telecommunications?

Perhaps we can arrive at an estimate by historical analogy. Take

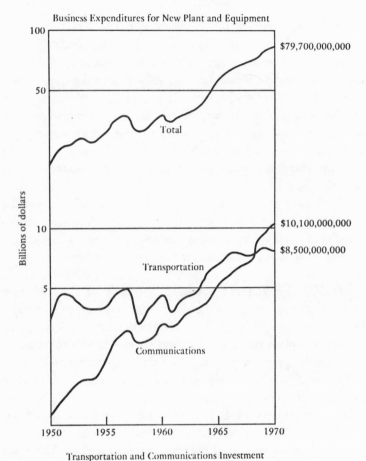

Business Expenditures for New Plant and Equipment

$79,700,000,000

$10,100,000,000

$8,500,000,000

Total

Transportation

Communications

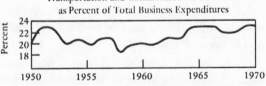

Transportation and Communications Investment
as Percent of Total Business Expenditures

Top: *Investment in communications (mostly in telephone plant) during
the period 1950–1970 increased more rapidly than investment in transportation.* Bottom: *Investment in communications and transportation
remained a constant proportion of total investment, suggesting that some
substitution of communications has been occurring.*

the trillion-dollar 1971 GNP and the 1971 investment in telephone plant (which amounted to about 80 billion dollars) and translate them into constant (1958) dollars. After this adjustment we have an economy of about 750 billion dollars and a telephone plant worth about 60 billion.

Now, how far back in United States history do we have to go to find a GNP of 60 billion dollars? The attributions of value become imprecise before 1920, so we can't pin it down to a specific year. But at some point between 1890 and 1900, the United States had a 60-billion-dollar economy (in 1958 dollars). Thus it has taken about eighty years starting in 1890, when AT&T began work on its telephone plant, to build a voice network that is worth as much as the whole economy's output in 1890.

So if we're talking about building a video plant that will cost as much as the 1971 GNP, it's clear that it won't be done overnight. If history is any guide, the kind of electronic network blithely assumed by the dispersal enthusiasts will not be built within the next twenty years, and probably not within the next thirty or forty.

INSTITUTIONAL LAG Although the technical and economic constraints on a nationwide video network are substantial, I believe that they are soluble in the long run. It is the political and institutional problems that remain forbidding.

Again, let's look at history. In 1967 the United States should have started using satellites for domestic telecommunications transmission over distances of more than 1,100 miles. That's when satellites became more economic than terrestrial facilities. But we didn't begin to use them for domestic telecommunications until seven years later. The delay was not due to any technological or economic problem; it was simply that we couldn't solve the political and institutional problems. Who was to own the system? Who would get what share of the revenues? Our inability to answer these questions delayed exploitation of a useful technology for seven years.

The same is true of cable television. Any new technology causes institutional conflicts, and the conflicting interests result in delayed benefits, delayed use of the technology.

The difficulties raised by the specialized telecommunications carriers are even more serious institutional barriers to dispersed settlement. The specialized carriers and the interconnect industry have generated numerous rate-making problems that could be the most critical obstacle to attaining dispersed settlement patterns in the future.

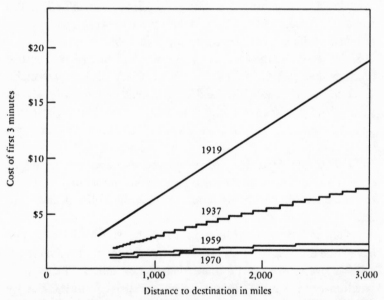

Long-distance telephone charges, 1919–1970. The cost of long-distance telephone calls dropped sharply between 1920 and 1970, making information transmission and the diffusion of knowledge increasingly independent of distance.

As illustrated by the graph of long-distance charges, the clear trend in telecommunications rate making has been toward lower rates and toward a flattening of the cost curve with distance. In facilities such as wide area telephone service (WATS) we enjoy, in fact, flat-rate service.

Marginal cost pricing, or some other nonaveraged pricing scheme, will certainly feed back into settlement patterns by making it more expensive to call smaller, peripheral, out-of-the-way places, and less expensive to transmit information among the larger cities. This means a comparative disadvantage for peripheral localities and a comparative advantage for metropolitan centers.

Of course, the common carriers have no choice. Their market is concentrated in metropolitan centers. Given the selective competition from Microwave Corporation of America and from Datran, there's no alternative to abandonment of average cost pricing and adoption of some scheme of marginal cost pricing.

I'm worried about this, because I see it as foreclosing a settlement option. If we continue to rely heavily on information as a resource, and if we make it much more difficult to get information into and out of isolated or peripheral places, that tends to close off the dispersal option.

Working out the competition problems will be the Bell System's major worry over the next twenty years. And I think the situation is fairly dangerous because of the principles that govern connecting networks. Networks have common properties, so that we can talk about the postal network, the telephone network, bus networks, and rail networks in the same way. In a fully articulated network some routes are always more profitable than others; some may even run at a loss. This does not mean, however, that the less profitable or unprofitable routes are not necessary and important to the network. They aggregate customers for more profitable routes, and they contribute to the general effectiveness of the network as a whole. If a link is removed or made more expensive at any location in a network, the effects reverberate throughout the system.

In connecting networks, every place is connected to every other. Improving or reducing service on any one link affects every link.

This is a critical property of random-access networks, and it is also evident in the value of networks. Part of the value of a telephone in New York City is that it can be used to call Lame Deer, Montana, or any other place. If it becomes more difficult to call Lame Deer, a New York City telephone is worth less.

The serious problem is that a positive and a negative cycle have historically affected interconnecting networks, and there's no reason to think that the telephone network is any different. There is a positive cycle in which, for some indeterminate period, you can provide better service at lower cost. Because the cost is lower and the service is better, you get more patrons. If you have more patrons you have more revenue, which means you can provide even better service at lower prices, and so it goes.

But there is also a negative cycle. If you must reduce service or raise rates, patronage declines. Then the cost of the network must be spread over fewer customers, and that means higher prices, which means reduced patronage—and down you go. Several familiar networks have gotten themselves into negative cycles. Rail passenger service certainly did. When the auto became popular and fewer people rode trains, railroad managers eliminated peripheral routes and raised fares. That drove more customers to competitive forms of transportation, and the system deteriorated rapidly. Local public transportation is in the same bind in many cities. The postal service has also passed from the positive to the negative cycle, and it will continue to lose money whether it's a corporation or a government operation. The cycle is inexorable once it starts.

So the next twenty years will be a critical time for the telephone industry. Either integrated communications will be maintained, or they will be reestablished in the same general way that an integrated railroad network was finally achieved. Many different lines were originally built at many different gages in different parts of the United States, and in the 1880s and 1890s the network was rationalized at a common gage. It seems to me that the communications situation which is developing is directly analogous. The competitive and fractionalized communications utilities will eventually require integration and rationalization. In the process some networks—possibly including the voice telephone network—could find themselves trapped in the negative cycle.

I believe that preserving the dispersal option depends on the maintenance of price averaging, and price averaging depends in turn on integrated, noncompetitive telecommunications networks.

A FORECAST

Gazing into the future of our settlement structure, I don't believe that cities will disappear into the countryside, even if the dispersed, communications-based option is preserved. What is technologically possible, economically feasible, and institutionally acceptable is not necessarily socially and culturally desirable, and dispersal may well be less popular than the enthusiasts have led us to expect. Moreover, just as it is a basic physical law that every action has an equal and opposite reaction, every social and geographical trend creates its own negative side effects. If there's one thing we should have learned from the previous settlement eras we've lived through, it is that machines are never trouble-free solutions to any problem. Telecommunications and settlement dispersal would, in the final analysis, only enable us to substitute one set of problems for those we currently face.

Thinking along these lines, I feel less certain of the evolution of a dispersed settlement pattern than some of the analysts I quoted. The fact that we have dispersed somewhat in the past does not guarantee that we will continue to disperse in the future, even if we have the option. And I feel even more pessimistic about the ability of advanced telecommunications or any other machine to solve the nation's settlement problems.

QUESTIONS AND ANSWERS

*You've discussed the problem of communication. Now, in the
new Hi-Lo Tariff, prices conform more closely to cost. An
economist might argue that efficiency is promoted by charging
higher prices to people who talk more. Are you advocating
an inefficient pattern of settlement in which the low-cost areas
actually subsidize the high-cost areas?*

First of all, I have problems talking to economists about networks.
I can only view networks as dispersed phenomena that extend all
over the United States and all over the world. An economist tends
to conceptualize networks as points. He adds up all the costs and
all the benefits for the network as a whole. He won't take it apart
in pieces. And I insist that if you talk about a network except in
pieces—except in terms of how this part interrelates with that part
—you're not talking about the network, you're talking about something else.

Now, as far as the question of efficiency versus inefficiency is
concerned, according to economic theory as it is practiced and
taught, there is subsidization. Under current rates the large cities
are subsidizing phone service for Lame Deer, Montana. Yes, I do
advocate that. I'm not convinced that the economist's marginal
cost pricing is always better than subsidy.

That satisfies me, and it may satisfy telephone people, but it
doesn't satisfy the economist and it doesn't satisfy the people down
at the Federal Communications Commission and the Office of
Telecommunications Policy who are listening to what the economists tell them. The problem is really an ideological one, and it's
difficult to fight it with logic. Experience has shown that a responsible, service-oriented, integrated utility is more efficient in the
broader social sense than competitive carriers. But if you're sold on
the idea that monopoly is always bad and competition is always

good, then no amount of logic is going to refute your belief that there should be more competition.

To combat such beliefs, I can only suggest some arguments. Shouting at each other all day wouldn't do any good. The arguments I would propose are based on the precept that every place in a network affects every other place. I would argue that raising the cost of telephone service between Bismarck and Fargo does affect New York City. I would say that before dismissing those effects, as the regulatory agencies have done, somebody ought to take a good look at them.

Secondly, I would cite a historical analogy. In the period before 1910, and in some cities after 1910, competitive local carriers were common. If a person wanted access to the entire telephone system he had to subscribe to two, and in some bizarre cases three, telephone systems. Everybody involved eventually agreed that this was a wasteful duplication of facilities, and that local telecommunications were a natural monopoly. And we've had a natural geographical monopoly of telecommunications ever since, except in rare cases. You don't have General Telephone & Electronics and one of the Bell operating companies competing for the same territory. Telephone service is indeed monopolistic, but it's a peculiar geographical monopoly.

If in the past it was demonstrated that competition doesn't make sense on a local scale, the argument that it doesn't make sense on a national scale now has great merit. For the national telephone system now operates in the way that local systems worked in 1910. One of the most striking discoveries I've come upon in looking at the history of telephone networks is that the city telephone network in year X is a virtually perfect predictor of the national network in year X + 20 or X + 30. Through more efficient communications techniques, we have shrunk the space of the United States. It's functionally equivalent today to what a metropolitan area was in 1910. And if it was senseless to have competitive carriers in a city, it's senseless to have competitive carriers on a national scale today.

> *I'd be the last person to argue for competition, but I've gotten the impression that you think dispersal is a good option. People who have made that value judgment have subsidized all kinds of inefficient social organizations. They've subsidized the networks that got us into this situation; they've subsidized passenger railroad traffic, which has helped produce some of these terrible commuting problems. Are you suggesting that in order to maintain a dispersed settlement option, we ought to continue average cost pricing? Wouldn't it be more efficient to let economics determine settlement patterns and charge people higher rates for the use of inefficient communications facilities, charge people for pollution, etc? We would then reinvigorate the city, which strikes me as a very good settlement pattern.*

Let me answer that in a couple of ways. First, yes, there is a value judgment on my part. I talked about dispersal as an option; I didn't talk about it as an optimum. And it's an option I want to preserve. Obviously, if we make information transmission very expensive, we help to foreclose the dispersal option.

With respect to whether dispersal itself is a good idea, I agree with you that metropolitan areas and cities are far more efficient human settlements than the dispersed settlements we've created by subsidizing highway users and commuter railroads at public expense. Moreover, if we were to try a very dispersed settlement pattern, we would probably create some serious problems.

Though there are enormous ecological difficulties caused by concentrating people in cities like New York, the ecological consequences of dispersing that population at a lower density could be even greater. To take an analogy, if we were to heat this podium to 5 million degrees Fahrenheit, the ecological effects would be negligible. If we spread the same amount of heat over the area of Pennsylvania, raising the average temperature by $1\frac{1}{2}$ degrees, the ecological effects would be comprehensive. It would change the climate, the vegetation, the runoff, the rainfall—everything. People who look upon dispersal as a solution to ecological problems are making some serious miscalculations. I think dispersal could exacerbate ecological problems as easily as solve them.

Besides, I'm committed to cities myself. There are many exciting experiences that are possible only in large metropolitan areas. We would certainly dilute some of the richness and variety of our lives by dispersing people hither and yon.

Finally, your suggestion that we let the economy take care of the settlement pattern may well be happening. In some respects the last several decades have been the most bizarre period in human history. The democratization of transportation since the cheap Model A is unprecedented; never before have individuals had such mobility. In making projections of what's going to happen in the future, we tend to look not at 1,000 or even 200 years of human history, but at the last 30 years. So we've come to think that increasing mobility is normal and will continue. The fact of the matter is, however, that the dizzy ride we've been on is coming to an end fairly quickly.

There's nothing on the drawing boards as revolutionary in terms of human settlement as freeway networks and automobiles. Urbanized areas have expanded about as far as they're going to; all the freeways have been built. Any urban freeway that doesn't exist now is not going to be constructed, because local opposition will block it. The mobility system available to individuals that enabled them to spread out is as good as it's going to get. Energy crunch aside, the invisible hand is operating.

Eventually, if there is widespread substitution of communication for transportation, there could be another dispersal cycle after a twenty-year period of stability. But my forecast for the next twenty years is very conservative with respect to human settlement. I think we'll see a settlement breather period comparable to the Depression and World War II, when city growth just stopped for about fifteen years.

Will you comment on the long-run future in reference to Walter Cronkite's "21st Century," which asserted that at some point in the future we will have to have electronic communities instead of commuter trains?

I don't believe it, for reasons which have to do with cultural obstacles to the substitution of communication for transportation. We can try to estimate what sorts of communications could be conducted with a picture-phone or over an electronic blackboard. But we're operating in a vacuum, because we don't know enough about human communication. I have a feeling that even if we get the most sophisticated media available, they will not be satisfactory substitutes for face-to-face communication. And to the extent that face-to-face communication is still important, we're not going to substitute electronic communication for commuting and we're not going to disperse.

Face-to-face communication is valued in all cultures, especially for negotiation and supervision. Man's entire communication history has been between people who were present in the flesh, and in delicate dealings there is still no adequate substitute. During the next twenty years we're not going to change a communications pattern which evolved over several thousand centuries.

The human face is a marvelously expressive communications instrument, as is the whole body. We pass signals back and forth with our bodies, especially with our faces. The face has the most complex musculature of any part of the body, and every inch of it communicates. It conveys things that we want people to know and sometimes betrays things we don't want them to know. When we're embarrassed, for example, many of us blush, no matter how hard we try not to.

In the little research that's been done in this area, psychologists and physiologists have found that the sensory ratio in communication is complex. Two people in conversation are sending and receiving relatively little data by voice. About 70 percent of the information they exchange is nonverbal. It consists of cues with the eyes, together with many other things like smell and temperature. Physiologists have recently discovered that we all emit odors which no amount of deodorant will cover up. They're not odors that we realize we're smelling; we perceive them unconsciously. All of us have had the experience of meeting a person whom we instantly like or dislike. It's becoming increasingly clear that one determinant of these intuitive reactions to people is unconsciously perceived odors.

Body temperature is also a communication medium. The cheek is excruciatingly sensitive to temperature changes. If a person tells you something you don't like, you get angry and your cheek temperature rises a tenth or a twentieth of a degree. At conversational distance, another person's cheek can detect this. This is reflected in our idioms: "The man made a heated remark," "She has a lot of cheek."

Such subtleties are important elements of face-to-face communications. Even if all the technical, economic, and institutional problems of electronic communication are solved, people may say, "So what?" I'm skeptical about Cronkite's "21st Century" for these reasons. Admittedly, it's largely an intuitive feeling, but the things I've been discussing support skepticism.

All the "revolutions" we hear about—communications, manufacturing, and so on—seem to me to have occurred gradually. Agriculture declined when manufacturing started, and communications started when the others diminished. Don't you think that dispersal will be the same? People will not stop living in cities, but some people will choose to disperse and others won't. Don't you think there's some future for large

*segments of the population to move off on their own, leaving
remnants of the city—just as we still have remnants of manufacturing in the communications era?*

Certainly I would agree. The fascinating thing about human history
is that mankind never loses anything completely. Because we have
747s, for example, doesn't mean we'll stop walking.

What we're trying to sort out is the ratio among trends and what
the ratio implies in terms of questions we should answer, machines
we should build, and policies we should adopt.

A small percentage of the population already lives in a dispersed
electronic communications wonderland. The President of the United
States does: wherever he is, he's tied in electronically. A few other
people command that kind of advanced communications technology, and we can certainly predict that their numbers will increase.

But the question I'm always interested in is the one about proportions: What fraction of the people do what, at what place, at
what time? Where will the bulk of the population be living, and
how will the bulk of the labor force be working, in X years? Is it
possible to take the 118 million people now in urbanized areas and
spread them over the land that we're not using? It's when you look
at the proportions that you can tell whether the trends you're focus-
ing on are significant.

*What is the role of the individual in this future pattern? Is it
one of just accepting or just rejecting it, without having much
real say about it?*

Here again we can talk about the ideal and the reality. Certainly
individuals should be giving their opinions to policy makers. But
to be realistic, a relatively small fraction of the population (5 or
10 percent) will react to policy questions. The majority of people
will reach a conclusion only when you present them with a concrete option.

The day the average Manhattan office worker discovers that it's possible for him to move to Morris County, New Jersey, commute to his job in New York City one day a week, and communicate electronically the rest of the time, he's going to decide whether to move or not. Until individuals are faced with realistic choices in terms that they understand, they will not form opinions on what options they prefer. Until then the executives who run large corporations, government regulatory agencies, banks, and so forth are the ones who will design policy.

The fact that most people need concrete options makes research on substituting communication for transportation very difficult. If you ask someone what he would do if he had a certain machine, he can't really tell you because he's never had it. You've got to give him the machine and let him play around with it; then he'll find out what he can do with it and what he can't.

You said that network growth and decline are irreversible cycles. Do you think cities are in the negative cycle, and if they are, do you think it can be reversed?

Some cities are in the negative cycle. St. Louis is an example; I doubt if that central city will ever be rejuvenated. But your question must be answered on an individual basis. Chicago, for instance, is not in a negative cycle. The key seems to be the executive community and their attitudes about the city. Consequently the migration of corporate headquarters out to the suburbs does not bode well. If the chairman of AT&T notices something outrageous on the way in to his New York office, he's in a position to call up City Hall and say, "Take care of this!" And something will probably be done. But if he and lots of other people like him don't have to come downtown anymore, there's nobody powerful to complain if things go wrong. And when there are no powerful people complaining about outrageous conditions, they persist.

I would suggest that the negative and positive cycles you've described are closed systems which don't have any external inputs, that the cycles therefore don't necessarily apply to open systems. The New York Telephone Company, for example, got itself into a negative cycle. It's clear that if the company had had to rely purely on its own earnings, it could not have extricated itself. The service got bad, the Public Service Commission refused rate increases because of the bad service, et cetera. But solid infusions of funds (on the average of 1 billion dollars a year) from elsewhere in the Bell System helped reverse the cycle. Logic suggests that the negative cycle New York City and St. Louis find themselves in is caused by political decisions that make the city subsidize the noncity. New York City income subsidizes highways that despoil the environment of New York, and so on. If there were ever the appropriate political will or determination in the country as a whole, then we could reverse this trend in the cities and generate an inverse transfer of money.

I agree fully, with one reservation: We have to know what to do. In the case of New York Telephone, I think it was fairly clear what had to be done.

You wouldn't have thought so if you had been there at the time!

Well, I'll say the fact that it has obviously been turned around is evidence that somebody knew, or quickly found out, what to do.

If we understand very little about communications, we know next to nothing about how people live in cities. For all the billions that have been poured into cities in urban renewal programs, and for all the research that's been funded, we are still basically ignorant about urban processes. We don't even know what cities mean to people. So of course we don't know how to intervene in urban processes in ways that will produce the results we want. The urban system is a black box.

Now, if I can plug the study I've just been working on, the Comparative Metropolitan Analysis Project was set up to look at what's going on in twenty American metropolitan systems. This may sound like a simple notion, but it's never been done before. Nobody has compared New York's experience with that of Baltimore, Houston, and so on. And of course, they are very different.

The difficulty with attempts at external intervention is that policy makers have not accommodated this diversity. External inputs come largely from the federal government, which tends to legislate as if all cities were the same. The urban committees in the House and Senate are dominated by people from the large metropolitan areas of the East, and they tend to think of national urban problems in terms of New York City's problems. Yet the housing and redevelopment legislation that makes lots of sense for New York doesn't work very well in Minneapolis, and may not work at all in Los Angeles. Until we resolve such issues, massive inputs into cities from the outside are likely to do more harm than good.

To conclude, I would emphasize that the same principle holds for the nation's telephone network. Specialized common carriers and the federal regulatory agencies have launched a major intervention into the operations of the nation's telecommunications network without considering whether they understand its intricate workings well enough to intervene successfully. In 1974, for example, the Federal Communications Commission decided to inquire into the social and economic effects of specialized competition—a decision that came several years *after* competition was launched. As is the case with many of our attempts to tinker with urban processes, the nation would be better off in the long run if we had taken the time to acquire a basic understanding of the ways the economy, society, and telecommunications interact *before* we permitted outside intervention in the form of fundamental changes in telecommunications policy.

SELECTED WRITINGS OF RONALD ABLER

"Distance, Intercommunications, and Geography," *Proceedings of the Association of American Geographers,* 3 (1971), pp. 1–4.

"The Geography of Communications," in Michael E. Eliot Hurst (ed.), *Transportation Geography: Comments and Readings,* McGraw-Hill, New York, 1974, pp. 327–346.

Human Geography in a Shrinking World: A Geography of the Future (editor, with Donald Janelle, Allen Philbrick, and John Sommers), Duxbury, North Scituate, Mass., 1975.

"Monoculture or Miniculture: The Impact of Communications Media on Culture in Space," in David A. Lanegran and Risa Palm (eds.), *Invitation to Geography,* McGraw-Hill, New York, 1973, pp. 186–195.

Spatial Organization: The Geographer's View of the World (with John S. Adams and Peter Gould), Prentice-Hall, Englewood Cliffs, N.J., 1971.

"What Makes Cities Important," *Bell Telephone Magazine,* March-April 1970, pp. 10–15.

THE COMING
OF THE
GOLDEN AGE
The Impact of Science on Human Affairs

ROBERT JASTROW

Robert Jastrow is the founder and director of the Institute for Space Studies, a New York branch of NASA's Goddard Space Flight Center. He is also professor of geophysics at Columbia University and professor of earth science at Dartmouth College.

Jastrow was born in New York and educated at Columbia, where he received his Ph.D. in physics in 1948. In the next ten years he was a fellow at Leiden University in the Netherlands, a member of the Institute for Advanced Study at Princeton, a research associate at the University of California, and assistant professor of physics at Yale. He joined NASA when it was formed in 1958 and served as chairman of its lunar exploration committee from 1959 to 1961. In 1961 he established the Institute for Space Studies, which sponsors research in astronomy, meteorology, and earth resources.

S CHOLARS who study the impact of science and technology on human affairs usually think of nuclear weapons as the most consequential product of the scientific revolution. Yet this development has not made a qualitative change in the way that nations conduct war, although it has changed the scale of potential destruction. The role of war as an instrument of foreign policy is much as it was two, three, and four thousand years ago. I believe that the impact of science has been more fundamental in other areas of thought and activity.

The first area concerns the past, and the second concerns the future. Regarding the past, science has provided a new version of Genesis, and a new understanding of the relationship between a human being and the world around him. Science has provided a special kind of answer to the questions: "What am I; how did I arrive on this planet; and what is my place in the cosmos?"

A NEW VERSION OF GENESIS

This story is an alternative to the first page of the Book of Genesis. It has no moral or ethical content. It is a story, or myth if you wish, derived from circumstantial evidence that developed out of the labors of many astronomers and biochemists working in their specialized fields during the last several decades.

FIREBALL According to this version of Genesis, the Universe began about 13 billion years ago as a dense, hot, compressed state of matter expanding rapidly outward—a kind of fireball. In the course of time as it expanded, it gradually became cool enough so that the forces of gravity acting on hydrogen, the primordial stuff of the Universe, caused it to condense into clouds. First, clouds the size of the galaxies formed, and then within these clouds further condensations produced individual stars. This began happening at the time the Universe was about 100 million years old, and it is still going on. About 4.6 or 4.7 billion years ago the star which became our sun condensed. As minor accompaniments to the condensation of the sun, nine smaller bodies formed, none of them big enough to burn hydrogen at their centers and be stars themselves. These were the nine planets of the solar system.

When the solar system formed, the Universe had existed for about 8½ billion years. Myriad stars, usually with families of planets around them, formed before our solar system existed, and stars with families of planets have formed many times since.

We can observe stars developing in the sky today; we can see the little black cloudlets of newly condensed matter. We have reason to believe that some stars near us have planets. In fact, it seems that planets and multiple condensations of the kind I described are the rule and not the exception.

There are 100 billion stars in our Galaxy, most of them accompanied by families of planets. There are 10 billion similar galaxies in the observable Universe. This means that 10^{21} stars, probably accompanied by families of planets, potentially exist there.

EARTHLIKE PLANETS   In the pursuit of the scientific version of Genesis the question immediately arises: What is the likelihood that some of these planets are inhabited? Behind this question lies another: What is the probability that life will develop on a suitable earthlike planet?

Not all the planets in the Galaxy and in the Universe resemble the Earth. Some must be like Mercury, which is not hospitable, or Jupiter, which has a very bizarre climate. But just as three planets out of nine in this solar system are earthlike—namely the Earth, Mars, and Venus—you might expect that 10 or 20 or 30 percent of the planets scattered around the Universe also are earthlike.

What is the chance that life will develop on such an earthlike planet? This brings us to the question: How did life appear on our planet? And it seems to me that there are only two possible answers.

Either life appeared here by an act of special creation, or it evolved out of nonliving chemicals. These exhaust the logical alternatives; there is no third way.

The first answer—an act of creation—puts the question outside the domain of science. If we wish to look for a scientific explanation to the question of the origin of life, we must restrict ourselves to the second alternative.

Suppose, then, that life evolved out of nonliving chemicals. The question now becomes: What is the mathematical chance that out of this humble beginning, a chain of evolution would develop that stretches from molecules to man?

That chain of events is surely extraordinary, even if it can be explained within the framework of scientific reasoning. It is entirely possible that the chance of its happening is as small as one in 10^{10} —one in 10 billion—in which case we are the only inhabited planet in our Galaxy. Or it may be as small as one in 10^{20}, in which case we are alone in the observable Universe. These probabilities are very small—so small that if they are correct, we might as well call life on our planet a miracle, or as close to a miracle as we can approach by a scientific chain of argument.

On the other hand, if the probability is even as large as, say, one in a million, there must be 100,000 inhabited planets in our Galaxy, and a thousand trillion inhabited planets in the observable Universe. That means we have many friends—or enemies—in the cosmos. It also means man's greatest experiences lie ahead of him.

It seems at first that we will never be able to find out the unknown probability—that we will never have the answer to the interesting question: Are we alone, or is our cosmos teeming with life? But suppose we discover remains of life, or even the beginnings of life, no matter how primitive, on a planet like Mars in this solar system. Then we will immediately know that the a priori probability of life evolving out of nonliving chemicals is *not* negligibly small. For if the chance of life evolving on a planet is as small as one in 10^{10} or one in 10^{20}, life would not have evolved by accident on *two* planets in the same solar system.

In fact, if a scrap of life—or even a strand of DNA barely on the threshold of life—should be found on Mars, we will know immediately that the chance of life evolving on an earthlike planet must be high. It must be roughly two-thirds, because two of the three earthlike planets in the solar system are inhabited by forms of life. Now, the statistics are poor when a sample of only three planets is involved, and two-thirds is not to be taken as an accurate statement of probability. Nonetheless, a probability as small as one in 10^{10} or one in 10^{20} would be eliminated by this discovery. We would know then that our Galaxy has millions, if not billions, of inhabited planets—that the Universe teems with life.

EXTRATERRESTRIAL SOCIETIES?   Remember that our solar system came into existence when the Galaxy and the Universe were already 8 or 9 billion years old, and that stars have been forming ever since. Some of the inhabited planets we are hypothesizing are billions of years older than we are, while some are billions of years younger. What kind of intelligence, communications, wisdom, or satisfaction might we find if we ever succeed in contacting these hypothesized extraterrestrial societies? What might we expect?

Consider the planets that are younger than we are. A billion years is a short period in the cosmic time scale, but in the history of life on Earth it is very long. Our fossil record of the past billion years is fairly complete, and the most advanced organisms that appear in the rocks of a billion years ago are only simple wormlike creatures. So if you go to another planet similar to the Earth, but a billion years younger, you cannot expect to find anyone to talk to. It is likely to be inhabited only by wormlike organisms and other zoological curiosities.

Now consider the planets formed a billion years before the Earth was born. Let us extrapolate into the future and imagine what kind of intelligent being might exist in such a planetary system. When we try to look that far ahead, we must remember that modern science has enormously accelerated the pace of change in human life. In this century no man dies in the same world to which he was born. That was never true before, and it emphasizes the fact that the application of intelligence to the control of our environment has produced a rapid acceleration of evolution. It is not an evolution of the shape and form of the body. It is cultural evolution, which progresses by leaps and bounds not through a change in the organism, but through the transmittal of learning from generation to generation.

Think of how our children will probably live in the year 2000, and how our descendants may be living in the twenty-first and twenty-second centuries. Then try and look ahead 1,000 years, 100 million years, a billion years. We have 6 billion years left in this solar system before the sun becomes a red giant and consumes the Earth. By then we will long since have fled to another part of the Galaxy; but we will probably stay on this planet for a billion years or more before leaving it forever.

What might another million or another billion years produce in our evolution? It is possible that in the further development of our species, mind and intelligence will be the sole focus and the body will become unimportant. There may be no substantial bodily form—flesh, muscle, and bone—for those intelligent organisms a million years in the future.

Following the same train of thought, extraterrestrial societies a billion years older than we are may be the essence of mind—streams and rivers of pure thought. They may be so advanced that we would not be of interest to them, and their intelligence probably could not communicate with ours. As our activities are mainly a mystery to our household pets, so the activities of such advanced beings may be a mystery to us. We may be permanently barred from communication with them, although their thoughts might be flowing through us and around us at all times.

This brings us as far out on the edge of speculation as I should like to go. But I believe that you must open your mind to these possibilities and watch carefully for signs of life on some other planetary body in our solar system. If that proof ever arrives, we will know that life is common, and we must be prepared for contact with highly evolved intelligences living on planets circling other stars.

SCIENCE AND HUMAN PRODUCTIVITY

The scientific version of Genesis is mainly of philosophical interest. The second major effect of science on human affairs has more practical consequences in everyday life. This is the increased productivity of human labor resulting from scientific discoveries—a development which is continuing without letup and which will eventually have the most serious repercussions.

Civilization began with a scientific invention called agriculture, which produced a food surplus for the first time and relieved some people from the necessity of dawn-to-dusk labor to feed themselves. As soon as that happened, society became organized into those who produced food and those who contributed other services. The increase in productivity mounted as new inventions accumulated. By 1900 our civilization had become very complex, and gains in productivity were increasing geometrically.

GOLDEN AGE OF LEISURE In 1900 the average workweek in this country was 60 hours. Today it is 40 hours and still shrinking; it may be heading toward 30. The average life span in the United States was 49 years in 1900, while today it is roughly 70 years and still increasing. The prospects for a 100-year life span in the next century are good, and it may be that 150 years or more is the ultimate lifetime that we can anticipate.

A long life and relief from dawn-to-dusk labor are great blessings. They mean more time for the family, for enjoyment, for cultivating the arts, for the liberation of the human spirit. But there is another side to this coin: As a species we have been fashioned by the patient pruning of natural selection to respond to environmental pressures. Over many millions of generations, the individuals who react best to these pressures have been the most likely to survive to maturity and leave progeny who inherit their desirable qualities. Thus a behavior pattern of response to challenges has been built into our genes. Most of us enjoy meeting the challenge of solving a problem, raising a family, doing a job, or whatever it may be—and whether we enjoy challenges or not, most of us begin to deteriorate without them. If we are to be denied the opportunity to exercise this fundamental human capability, the golden age of leisure may turn into a leaden age of boredom.

THE WORLD OF THE OYSTER So the subtlest but most destructive consequence of the application of science to human affairs is a productivity so great that the pressures of the environment would be removed for most people. The absence of pressure would mean that no force would act in each generation to favor one set of traits over another. All traits would become neutral. Evolution would halt, and so would change and progress.

It happened to the oyster 200 million years ago; that simple animal has not changed since then. But human beings have evolved explosively. As we have filled our new niche, the fossil record shows that the brain has doubled in size in the last million years. It is the most rapid and explosive growth of an organ that biologists have found.

The brain is not growing any more, and has not for the last 100,000 years. We have become fully adapted to our environmental niche as the thinking animals. What does the future hold for us? The static world of the oyster? Or a golden age of continued progress and fulfillment?

Based on the history of the oyster, the prospects are grim. I think there will be only one avenue to further growth as we move into the twenty-first century. And that requires a change in the values of our society in the direction of lifelong education. Such a development would make it possible for an active person to have not one or two, but three or four careers in his lifetime, with a change in career every thirty or forty years.

Although continuing education would be integral to such a society, it need not take place in the classroom. No one has much taste for going back to school in the conventional sense. Instead there could be a system of universities without walls, perhaps based on communications satellites and the equivalent of cable television that would bring broad-band information into every home. It would entail a transformation of our society, because at the present time we do not esteem adult education highly enough to pay the cost of lifelong schooling. I do believe, however, that our recognition of the necessity for change, together with wise leadership, can bring us into the golden age.

EVOLUTION AND THE COMPUTER

I should like to mention one speculation on the future evolution of man that has particular interest for me as a technician and scientist. There has been a tenfold increase in electronic computing speed, and a tenfold decrease in computing power needs, every seven years since the first generation of computers, starting with Univac in 1952. We are now in the fourth computer generation—the era of the microcircuit "chip," the integrated circuit—which is accelerating this development. A conservative extrapolation of computer technology to the end of the century, bringing us to the eighth generation, suggests that a computer containing 10 billion neurons, which can match the human brain in raw thinking power, will exist in the same space and with the same power requirements as our largest computers today.

These intelligent machines will be constructed because we will need their help in managing the complex world of the twenty-first century. Programmer-tutors will spend perhaps ten years working with each machine, filling its memory with knowledge and basic skills and then developing its ability through a graded series of progressively difficult exercises. Eventually the machine's intelligence will resemble that of a highly trained human mind.

Artificial intelligences will begin to play a major role in the management of our economy, our corporations, our cities, our society. We will look to solid-state brains for specialized but exceedingly thorough explorations of complex possibilities that cannot be matched by the human brain. We will need them badly for this management counsel. Consequently we will be living in a kind of symbiotic union with these organisms.

You may look down on electronic brains because they are not housed in flesh-and-blood containers. That would be a mistake, because they will be capable of sophisticated, complex value judgments. If we wish to teach them aesthetics, they will have a very good aesthetic sense—and perhaps some moral sense, if we want to teach them that. They will be formidable partners for the human manager in the twenty-first-century world.

Remember that the human brain is no longer increasing in size. People will not change very much in the next century, but the computer is still evolving at an explosive rate; it has not reached anything like the limits of its capability. What will happen to it in the twenty-second century, the twenty-third, the thirtieth? And where will the human race be, one thousand or ten thousand years from now? What will be the ultimate products of the evolution of intelligence on this planet? Will they be flesh and blood, or will they be solid-state? These are some of the possibilities that we should keep in mind as we watch the development of circuit chip technology.

QUESTIONS AND ANSWERS

How can we cope with the impact of the products of science when society does not yet have the wisdom to control these applications?

I think that safety lies in preserving the government institutions in this country. They have protected us so far, and they will continue to protect us as long as we maintain a sound balance of powers and a strong free press. In my view, with the protection of these institutions we will be able to cope with any irresponsibility that individual citizens may subject us to.

Do you think man will ever attain so much knowledge that he has to leave this planet in order to challenge his curiosity?

I believe we will leave this planet because I think that the mind and the spirit grow on new experiences. There will come a day when the 30 billion acres that make up the surface of the Earth no longer hold surprises for us. We will have to reach out for new experiences or else accept stagnation.

We may leave the planet physically, as science fiction writers keep suggesting. Perhaps we will travel in space arks the size of the Queen Mary that carry 5,000 men and women—a microsociety whose members have finite life spans but whose life span as a society is infinite. Or we may stay here and enlarge our experience by entering into the nervous system of the Galaxy through communication. One or the other, I should think.

Will you review some of our efforts to establish communication with other planets?

There aren't any. We are listening all the time to radio impulses from the stars, and so far we have heard no patterns that could be construed as signals rather than random radiation. Plans have been outlined for beaming signals in the direction of a dozen or so nearby stars. But implementing the plans would cost hundreds of millions of dollars, and our species is not yet curious enough about the Galaxy to spend the money.

If we get through this valley of despair—this interval when we don't know how to control our nuclear weapons—and enter into a stable period, we will decide to make that investment. But it won't happen in this century.

The Book of Ezekiel describes what might be the landing of a spacecraft:

> "And behold, a whirlwind came out of the north, a great cloud, and a fire enfolding itself, and a brightness was about it, and out of the midst thereof as the color of amber, out of the midst of the fire."

And it goes on to talk about the winged creatures who appeared from the brightness. Clarke and Kubrick's scenario in *2001* seems plausible to me; it may be that a planet like ours is visited occasionally by beings who are waiting for signs that we're worth talking to. I don't think there's evidence for it, but I believe we should keep our minds open to the possibility.

SELECTED WRITINGS OF ROBERT JASTROW

"Are We Alone in the Cosmos?" *Natural History Magazine*, May 1974.

Astronomy: Fundamentals and Frontiers (with Malcolm H. Thompson), 2nd ed., Wiley, New York, 1974.

"How Old Is the Universe?" *Natural History Magazine*, August-September 1974.

Introduction to *The Next 10,000 Years* by Adrian Berry, Saturday Review Press, New York, 1974.

"Man in Space or Chips in Space," *New York Times Magazine*, Jan. 31, 1971.

"The Moon Is Still a Generally Silent Witness," *New York Times News of the Week in Review*, March 24, 1974, p. 7.

The Origin of the Solar System (editor, with A. G. W. Cameron), Academic Press, New York, 1963.

Red Giants and White Dwarfs: The Evolution of Stars, Planets and Life, 2nd ed., Harper & Row, New York, 1971.

INDEX

Abler, Ronald, 155
Air Quality Act, 147
air pollution and automobile, 133
  see also environment
Ash Commission, 147
authority, decline in late capitalism, 8–9
automobile
  and environment, 133–134
  and traffic safety, 16–19
  weight and fuel consumption, 133
Automobile Safety Act, 147

Bacon, Roger, 118
Bagge, Carl E., 143
Bell, Alexander Graham, 72, 118
Bell, Daniel, 65
Bell Laboratories, 119
Bell System, 12, 14, 25, 116, 119, 167, 178
Berry, Brian, 161
blacks
  migration and changing life styles, 73–74

unemployment, 87
and urban crisis, 48, 51
Boswash, 73
business
  dialogue with American polity, 3–4
  and government, adversary relationship, 1–5
  limits of responsibility, 19–21
  and power, 39–40
  public opinion of, 9–11
  and urban crisis, 61
  utilitarian, vs. normative institutions, 13–15

Campaign GM, 19
capitalism
  late, decline of authority in, 8–9
  late-late, 15–19
  liberal-democratic, 2–3
  and liberty, 20
  nationalism and decline of, 11–12
Capitalism, Socialism, and Democracy (Schumpeter), 11

Chase Manhattan Bank, 93
child labor, 31
Chippits, 73
cities
  concentration of people in, 156
  crisis in, 46–47
  and energy crisis, 140
  factories and employment in,
    48–49, 51
  and mass transit, 53–54
  minorities in, 87
  and regulated industries, 146–
    147
  social classes in, 46–47
  stasis in, 56
Civil Rights Act, 146
Clean Air Act (1970), 131, 135
coal
  and energy crisis, 134
  industry development, 137
Cohn, Harry, 17
Commission on Critical Choices
  for Americans, 130, 140–141
Comparative Metropolitan Analysis Project, 179
computer and evolution, 189–190
Congress, power in, 33–35
consumerism and regulated industries, 145
Corwin, Edward S., 34
costs
  of government, 78
  health care, 92–93
  and needs of environment, 114–
    115
Council of Economic Advisers, 68
Cromwell, Oliver, 35
Cronkite, Walter, 174, 175

David, Edward E., 162

democracy
  defined, 28
  existential limit on control, 34
  and majority power, 35–38
  and power of choice, 42–43
  and power to revolt, 29–30
  vs. totalitarianism, 37–38
Diamond, Henry L., 129
DiSapio, Carmine, 15
Drucker, Peter F., 111
Duke Power Co., 91
Dulles, John Foster, 41
Du Pont de Nemours, E. I. & Co.,
  Inc., 76

Earth Day, 130
ecologic man, 150–151
economy
  interdependence, 67–68
  and productivity of knowledge
    workers, 114
Edison, Thomas A., 118
education
  of labor force, 86
  and race relations, 32
Eisenhower, Dwight D., 42
energy
  crisis in cities, 140
  and environment, 130–136
  and price regulation, 137
  solid waste as source of, 134–
    135
  thermal vs. solar, 138–139
entitlements
  and changing social values, 76–
    77
  and communal society, 70–71
environment
  and automobiles, 133–134
  and ecologic man, 150–151

needs and costs, 114–115
and offshore oil drilling, 131
and oil shale, 132
and strip mining, 131–132
and sulfur in fuel, 131
environmentalism and regulated industries, 145
Etzioni, Amitai, 13
evolution
and computer, 189–190
and scientific advances, 188–189
externalities, and communal society, 70

Federal Communications Commission, 151, 170, 179
Federalist Papers, 30
Federal Meat Inspection Act, 147
Federal Power Commission, 145, 146, 151, 152
Federal Trade Commission, 8, 151
Federal Water Pollution Act (1972), 131
Federal Water Pollution Control Act, 135
feudalism and organizational power, 39–40
Flammable Products Act, 147
foreign policy, executive branch superiority in, 34
Freedom of Information Act, 146
Friedman, Milton, 20
The Futurist, 161

Galbraith, John Kenneth, 17, 24
General Motors Corp., 21, 39, 40
General Telephone & Electronics, 171
Ginzberg, Eli, 85

Goethe, Johann Wolfgang von, 66
Goldwater, Barry, 28
Gompers, Samuel, 91
government
and business, adversary relationship, 1–5
and congressional power, 33–35
costs, as social problem, 78
expenditures for ineffectual programs, 60–61
housing expenditures, 60–61
and majority power, 35–38
policy, and public opinion, 40–42
and power to revolt, 29–30
regulatory legislation, 147–148
and urban crisis, 52–53
Grapes of Wrath (Steinbeck), 54
groups
changing composition, 72–76
leadership and morale, 99

Haddon, William, 16
Harriman, Averell, 16
health care costs, 92–93
housing
government expenditures for, 60–61
integration, and soical class, 50
How to Talk Back to Your Television Set (Johnson), 161
Humphrey, Hubert, 28

inflation and post-industrial society, 75–76
information, freedom of, and regulatory agencies, 146
innovation and institutions, 116–119

institutions
  and innovation, 116–119
  and knowledge workers, 124–127
  normative vs. utilitarian, 13–15
  policy changes needed, 90
intelligence testing, ruling on, 91
Interstate Commerce Commission, 18, 39

Jastrow, Robert, 181
Jefferson, Thomas, 29
job enrichment, 121
Johnson, Lyndon, 28
Johnson, Nicholas, 161

Kahn, Herman, 75
Kahn's law, 75
Kennedy, John F., 18
knowledge workers
  in institutionalized world, 124–127
  and managers, 120–124
  productivity measurement, 113–116
  unskilled, 112
  see also labor force
Kristol, Irving, 45

labor force
  agricultural, 92
  education, 86
  pension vesting, 89
  productivity, and technology, 92–93
  and security on the streets, 90–91
  unemployment, 86–87, 89
  women in, 87–88
  and work environment, 91

see also knowledge workers
labor unions
  decline of confidence in, 10
  and modern society, 31–32
leadership and morale, 99
leisure and scientific advances, 187–188
liberty and capitalism, 20
Lincoln, Abraham, 118
Lockheed Aircraft Corp., 40

majority, power in, 35–38
managers
  in institutionalized world, 126–127
  and knowledge workers, 120–124
Mankiewicz, Herman J., 17
Marx, Karl, 11
Maxwell, Clark, 72
media
  impact of, 62–64
  Schumpeter on role of, 23
Mencken, H. L., 14
Menninger, W. Walter, 97
Metternich, Prince von, 13
Microwave Corp. of America, 167
middle class
  exodus from cities, 56–58
  and urban crisis, 48, 50
military
  ex-officers in job market, 124
  morale factors, 98–100
  slump of confidence in, 9–10
minorities in cities, 87
morale
  curve applications, 110
  lessons from the military, 98–100
  Peace Corps, 101–110

Morgenthau, Hans J., 27
Moynihan, Daniel P., 7, 69

Nader, Ralph, 18
National Environmental Policy Act (1969), 132
New Deal and national society, 67–68
New York Telephone Co., 87, 178
New York Times, 47, 50, 63
Nixon, Richard, 28

Office of Telecommunications Policy, 170
oil drilling, offshore, and environment, 131, 134
oil shale and environment, 132, 134
organization, normative vs. utilitarian, 13–15
overload, as social problem, 79

Pacific Gas & Electric, 149
patrician class
    and mass transit, 53–54
    and urban crisis, 47–49
Peace Corps
    crisis of arrival, 101–105
    crisis of engagement, 105–109
    crisis of reentry, 109–110
pension vesting, 89
Pearcy, G. Etzel, 68n
Pierce, John R., 162
Pipeline Safety Act, 147
planets
    communication with, 191–192
    earthlike, 183–185
    extraterrestrial societies on, 185–187

politics
    and changing social values, 76–77
    participatory, and regulated industries, 145–146
    utilitarian approach to, 15
pollution, *see* environment
population
    concentration in cities, 156
    dispersal, and telecommunications, 159–162
    shifts, 73
    and social problems, 80–81
power
    of choice, 42–43
    in Congress, 33–35
    in majority, 35–38
    in organizations, 39–40
    to revolt, 29–30
President's Council on Recreation and National Beauty, 145
pressure groups and political decision making, 82
productivity
    innovation and institutions, 116–119
    measurement, for knowledge workers, 113–116
    and science, 187–189
    and technology, 92–93
professional-technical class, 74–76
public opinion
    of business, 9–11
    and government policy, 40–42

quality of life, and changing social values, 77

race relations and modern society, 32

rationalism and decline of capitalism, 11–12

regulated industries, structural changes in, 148–150

regulatory agencies
institutional developments, 144–150
procedural developments, 152
substantive developments, 150–152

revolution and government, 29–30

Rockefeller, Laurance, 140, 145

Rockefeller, Nelson, 140

Roosevelt, Franklin D., 67, 68

Rubens, Peter Paul, 117

Samuelson, Paul, 19

San-San, 73

schools, integration vs. community control, 52

Schumpeter, Joseph, views on decline of capitalism, 11–12, 20, 23

science and human productivity, 187–189

second careers for knowledge workers, 123–124

settlement
eras, 156–159
forecast, 169
and telecommunications, 159–169

shortages as social problem, 78–79, 81–82

Smith, Adam, 2

Smithsonian, 68

Snow, C. P., 24

society
communal, 69–71
decision making in, 31–33

national, 67–69

normative vs. utilitarian, 13–15

post-industrial, 71–72; and inflation, 75–76

power relationships vs. authority relationships, 8–9

solar energy, 139

solid waste, as energy source, 134–135

Southern California Edison, 149

Southern Interstate Nuclear Board, 149

stasis in cities, 56

states, and national society, 68–69

Steinbeck, John, 54

strip mining and environment, 131–132

sulfur in fuel, and environment, 131

Supreme Court vs. majority rule, 37

tariff, Hi-Lo, 170

technology
and productivity, 92–93
speed of travel, 118

telecommunications
capital investment, 163–165
hardware, 162–163
institutional lag, 165–169
and settlement, 159–169

thermal energy, 138

totalitarianism vs. democracy, 37–38

traffic safety and automobiles, 16–19

transportation
and settlement, 158–159, 160
as urban problem, 53–54

Trollope, Anthony, 117
2001 (film), 192

unemployment, national vs. local,
    86–87
U.S. Steel Corp., 39, 40
universe
    and earthlike planets, 183–185
    and extraterrestrial societies,
        185–187
    fireball as beginning of, 182–
        183
urban crisis
    and government, 52–53
    and patrician class, 47–49
    see also cities
urban renewal, conflict of social
    classes over, 48
Utah Power and Light, 150

utilities, regional power pools,
    149–150

Vail, Theodore, 116
values, changing, 76–77
veto, in overturning majority de-
    cision, 37

Water Quality Act, 147
welfare
    blacks on, 73
    families on, 59–60
    national standards needed for,
        69
Wilson, Woodrow, 34
women in labor force, 87–88
work force, see labor force
working class, native-born, 74
workweek, four-day, 89

This book was edited by Mary Barnett and designed by Ben Kann.
Donald U. Honicky of AT&T supervised the project.
It was set by V & M Typographical, Inc.
The printer and binder was The Book Press, Inc.

DATE DUE
